Advanced Schutzhund

Advanced Schutzhund

By Ivan Balabanov
and Karen Duet

 Howell Book House
New York

Library of Congress Cataloging-in-Publication data

Balabanov, Ivan
Advanced schutzhund/by Ivan Balabanov and Karen Duet.
        p.   cm.
Includes bibliographical references.
ISBN 0-87605-730-X
1. Schutzhund (Dog sport) 2. Schutzhund dogs—Training.

Manufactured in the United States of America

05 06 07   8 7 6 5 4

Book Design: Holly Wittenberg
Cover Design: George McKeon

Dedication

To Lia (Nakita Des Deux Pottois, SchHIII, IPOIII, FH), my best friend.

Ivan and Lia at the 1994 USA Nationals, where she took High in Obedience. (Doug Loving)

And to Nana (Nany Des Deux Pottois, SchA, AD, BH), my little dynamo.

Nana with her Schutzhund A medal in 1992.

Contents

Foreword

When I was approached by Ivan Balabanov in the spring of 1998 to supply photographs for a new Schutzhund book he was writing with Karen Duet, I was both honored and pleased. It has been a privilege to observe and photograph Ivan and his little Belgian Malinois bitch Nakita Des Deux Pottois SchH III at National events since 1992. It is rare to observe a competitor at a Schutzhund trial that does not yell commands to his dog, who handles a dog that is so obviously full of love and respect for her handler and performs her heart out. Ivan's voice rarely rises past the volume of an intimate conversation with his dog; she works because she wants to please Ivan. If Ivan can share some of his training techniques with his readers, and those techniques are applied, we will surely be seeing happier, more spirited dogs on the competition field.

This book goes a bit further. For anyone considering the purchase of a dog for Schutzhund Sport, this book is a must. The chapters on selecting a new puppy or older dog will save the reader thousands of dollars and years of wasted time and heartbreak. What could be more discouraging than to pay thousands for a new dog or puppy, only to find as the dog matures that you don't have a dog capable of doing the work? This happens every day to trainers and novices worldwide. The evaluation techniques taught here will help you to make the best choice for a dog that you will share your life with.

In the training sections of this book, advanced training methods and techniques will show you how to build a positive, happy, willing spirit in your new dog or puppy and how to present a competition dog that will be exciting to handle and exciting for the spectators and judges to watch. Each portion of an exercise is broken down into the responsibilities of the dog and the handler, and what the judge wants and needs to see. The photographs that accompany the text will illustrate clearly what the handler should do to follow Ivan and Karen's directions. You will also find suggestions to clean up or fix a dog that has problems in any phase of the sport.

Finally, tips and techniques are offered to help the reader when all the hard work has paid off and you are going to compete with your well-trained dog. While most of this section of the book refers to National competitions, the advice offered here also applies to club trials and other events. In the excitement of a SchH Trial, common-sense errors occur and unexpected situations will always arise. Here, from experience, Ivan and Karen share their thoughts on trial preparation, ways to keep your dog focused and how to get the most from your dog once you hit the field with the world watching.

I've been in working dogs for 20 years and have spent thousands on seminars. I always felt I got my money's worth if *one new thing* was learned. I guarantee that you will learn more than one thing from reading this book. Even with all of my time with working dogs, I have changed small parts of my relationship with my dogs based on what I have read here, and I now understand a bit more about how they think.

I wish you good reading and better training, See you at the SchH Trial.

Douglas Loving

Introduction

When I was asked to put together a book on advanced Schutzhund several years ago, the task did not at first appear to be a difficult one. Having been involved with Schutzhund for several years, and having been a member of Schutzhund USA since 1991, I was familiar enough with the sport to write on the subject. I also knew that I was by no means an expert on the subject of advanced Schutzhund. This book would require a coauthor who had competed at the top levels of the sport (Nationals and Worlds) and who had coached others at this level.

In the process of looking for such a person, I ran across many people who had the experience but who lacked the ability to organize their thoughts into a method. It seems that many people know *what* they do, but few understand *why* they do it the way they do.

I also had difficulty finding an individual whose methods I could agree with ethically. I have always felt that training based in psychology, that strives to work with the dog's drives, desires, and abilities rather than *against* them, is the best and most natural form of training. There are times when force may be necessary, but in general I have found that positive reinforcement produces a much happier working dog. My challenge then became to find a coauthor who had the same basic belief and who had excelled in Schutzhund while using such techniques.

Ivan Balabanov was the man I was looking for. He has a well-defined style and an organized understanding of his method. Ivan's experience is immense. Because he grew up in Bulgaria, then lived in Belgium for several years and trained with the Germans, Belgians, French and Dutch, he has the benefit of having learned both Eastern and Western European methods. After moving to the United States, he opened his own training business and behavioral counseling center, and he is currently the director of the San Francisco SPCA Academy for dog trainers.

Ivan's style is a blend of all of the methods that he has learned over the years. His methods are *based* in operant conditioning but allow for many other psychological premises. I found Ivan to be a trainer who understands not only what methods he uses, but also why he uses them. He understands very well the results of all of his training methods on the spirit of the dogs he is working. Like a great artist, he picks his techniques judiciously and applies them carefully in order to get the most from his dogs. It is with great pleasure and satisfaction that I can bring you his methods in this book.

We would like you, the reader, to understand that we struggled with how to properly present this book to you. This book is written on the subject of *advanced* Schutzhund. We realize, however, that some readers will not be at the advanced level. In the first two chapters, we cover some basic ground in order to bring the less experienced reader up to speed on the subject. To those of you who are experts yourselves in the field, we ask for your understanding.

It is our hope that this book will further the understanding of what the sport is all about, and the training methods and dedication required to perform at the top levels of the dog sport known as Schutzhund.

Karen Freeman Duet

I want to thank Karen Duet for deciding to write this book with me, and especially Lori Nowell for helping me throughout this adventure. And Beth Adelman as well for being our editor!

Ivan Balabanov

The Spirit of Schutzhund

As we set out to write about the spirit of Schutzhund, the challenge was to put into words a *feeling*, an excitement—something that is real, but not quite tangible.

The *spirit*, after all, is associated with the soul. It is the mind and feelings, as distinguished from the body. The spirit is the real essence or significance of something, whether it is a human being or the European dog sport known as Schutzhund.

Translated from the German, *Schutzhund* means *protection dog*. While protection is definitely one of the three skills tested in the sport, the name has the potential to cause confusion. The sport equally involves the evaluation of tracking skills, obedience training and protection work, valuing balance above all in the dog's capabilities.

What Is Schutzhund?

Schutzhund is intended to demonstrate the dog's intelligence and utility. As a working trial, Schutzhund measures the dog's mental stability, endurance, structural efficiency, ability to scent, willingness to work, courage and trainability. Schutzhund is not meant to be personal

The true spirit of Schutzhund is the spirit of sport and teamwork. (Doug Loving)

protection training, although the skills are similar to those taught to police K-9s and security and protection dogs. Schutzhund is, first and foremost, a sport. The sport develops and evaluates traits in a dog that create a more balanced, happy and useful companion for its owners.

Those who are familiar with American Kennel Club (AKC) obedience trials and tracking tests will recognize the first two parts of Schutzhund because the tests have many similarities. The Schutzhund standards for the third part—protection work—are similar to those for dogs in police work. While not a test for police dogs or personal protection dogs, many Schutzhund dogs are later converted to one of these applications.

With this in mind, the spirit of Schutzhund could be described as "two working together as one." The dog and handler learn a routine that they practice in harmony with one another, each understanding the other's intent and body language. When performed at the highest levels, the bond between dog and handler is so great that the relationship is almost tangible.

Teamwork and Dedication

Because of the spirit and energy necessary for such a performance, it is our opinion that positive motivational techniques and training methods that are in harmony with the dog's natural drives will develop the ultimate dog and handler team. It is this type of positive motivational approach that we intend to put forward in this book. As with any "art," there are many methods and techniques used in training dogs. Some use more compulsion than others. While we acknowledge that aversion training does exist, it is our intention to put forward a method that is more harmonious with nature and that will remain effective over the long term.

Schutzhund is a sport enjoyed by people from all different walks of life—young and old, men and women, as well as people with disabilities. Although it started in Germany, several hundred thousand people from all over the world (currently, 17 countries) send teams to the world championships. The sport offers the participant the ability to test his or her training against that of other handlers and their dogs. It also forges new friendships and associations in the world of dog sports. One of the attractions of Schutzhund is that it is an outdoor sport that is both physically and mentally challenging. It is good exercise, fun and full of rewards.

As with any sport, Schutzhund requires dedication. This is not an eight-week training class, where a goal can be achieved in a short period of time and then dog and handler move on. No, Schutzhund requires a several-year commitment. A true Schutzhund competitor works with his or her dog and the club they belong to two to five times a week. The average age for a dog to achieve a Schutzhund I title is two and a half years. With the foundation work completed, some hard-working teams may then go on to achieve the Schutzhund III title by the time the dog reaches the age of three. It takes this long for all three elements of the equation to develop: training, conditioning and maturity of the dog.

If this team is going to compete seriously, Schutzhund III is only the beginning. At three years of age, the dog has just attained its black belt, to use a martial arts metaphor. The dog is usually not at the top levels of competition until about five or six years of age.

As you can see, Schutzhund is a sport that becomes a lifestyle. It takes years of training and dedication to get to the top levels. It is not just the dog that competes, but the handler as well. The two are a team that sets out to create the perfect dance together, to be in step with one another. When it is done correctly, it is beautiful to watch.

This book is about the *final* product in Schutzhund. It is about what sets the top competitors apart from those at the lower levels of the sport. It is about the polished performance and the theory that goes into making a top team at the national and world levels of competition.

If you are unfamiliar with Schutzhund, we refer you to the book *Schutzhund: Theory and Training Methods*, by Susan Barwig and Steward Hilliard, which is a good introduction to the sport and a prerequisite for reading this book.

This book is dedicated to all of the competitors who have devoted themselves to dancing with dogs, and to all of those dogs who have dedicated themselves to serving humanity. In the end, this is the spirit of Schutzhund.

Selecting and Raising the Schutzhund Candidate

Of all the decisions you must make in the process of reaching the top levels of Schutzhund competition, selecting the dog is the most important.

Most people understand that you cannot buy just any horse and expect it to run in the Kentucky Derby. Likewise, you cannot select just any dog and expect him to reach the top levels of Schutzhund competition. The dog you select must have the proper drives, good nerves, sound health and a balanced mind—just a few of the necessary attributes.

Your selection will be critical to your success. A very experienced trainer will tell you that they can apply the same training methods to 10 different dogs and get 10 different results. This is because dogs, like people, have their own personalities and will respond differently to things like correction, praise, stress, pain and excitement.

Which Breeds May Compete?

Each country has its own regulations regarding which breeds are allowed to compete in Schutzhund. In the United States, there are few Schutzhund organizations. United Schutzhund Clubs of America (USA)

5

Renee Lancaster's German Shepherd Dog at the 1995 USA North America in Albuquerque. (Doug Loving)

is the largest. It is a German Shepherd organization that allows other breeds to compete at its trials. There are also other breed-specific clubs that compete through USA.

LV/DVG America (*Deutscher Veband der Gebrauchshundsportverine*) is an international all-breed Schutzhund club with no specific breed requirements. Even mixed breeds are allowed to compete. This is a sport organization rather than a breed organization. DVG membership is divided into 13 regions; 12 are in Germany and the 13th is the United States. The winner of the DVG America Nationals qualifies to compete at the DVG Championship in Germany.

Clubs such as the United States Rottweiler Club (USRC), the United Belgian Shepherd Dog Association (UBSDA) and others host their own national and world championships. These breed clubs belong to the America Working Dog Federation (AWDF). The AWDF is currently working on becoming a full member of the Fédération Cynologique Internationale (FCI), which conducts all-breed world competitions held under IPO—the International Schutzhund rules.

Which Breeds May Compete?

The breeds that FCI allows to compete change each year. Below is the most current list of breeds, in alphabetical order:

Airedale	Briard
Anatolian Shepherd Dog	Bouvier des Flandres
Australian Kelpie (minimum 40–45 cm tall)	Boxer
	Doberman Pinscher
Australian Shepherd	German Shepherd Dog
Beauceron	Great Pyrenees
Belgian Shepherd (Groenendael)	Hovawart
	Picardie
Belgian Laekenois	Rottweiler
Belgian Malinois	Schnauzer (Giant and Standard)
Belgian Tervuren	
Border Collie	

Selecting a Breed

When you are deciding which breed to compete with in Schutzhund, keep in mind that the sport was originally designed as (and still is) a test for the German Shepherd Dog. Because of this, an agile and quick breed with a good nose, such as a German Shepherd, Belgian Malinois or other shepherd-type breed best performs the tracking, obedience and protection exercises. This is not to say that you cannot compete and score well with another breed. There are Australian Shepherds, Airedales and even Labrador Retrievers (just to name a few) that have earned titles with high scores. You may simply find it more of a challenge to train some breeds to the same level of performance.

Although many breeds can be trained in Schutzhund, the most popular breeds are the German Shepherd Dog, Belgian Malinois, Rottweiler, Doberman Pinscher, Giant Schnauzer and Bouvier des Flandres.

Looking through statistics from previous all-breed world championships, 50 percent of the competitors are German Shepherd Dogs and 35 percent are Belgian Malinois (a breed that has been rapidly growing in popularity in the last five years). Rottweilers, Doberman Pinschers, Giant Schnauzers and Bouvier des Flandres make up 10 percent of the remaining competitors, and 5 percent are breeds from the remainder of the FCI list.

It would be wise to speak to owners of the breed you are interested in to learn more about its character traits. Speaking with someone who has already been involved in Schutzhund with that breed may open your eyes to the pros and cons of your selection.

Puppy or Adult?

When purchasing a Schutzhund candidate, you have three choices:

1. A puppy that you raise and train yourself (or with the help of a club) to the top level of competition;
2. A young, green dog (untrained or with little training) obtained at 8 to 18 months of age;
3. An imported or domestic Schutzhund-titled dog.

There are pros and cons to each of these choices.

*Viki Bartley's Australian Shepherd Scrap's Rusty Lugar, SchHIII, with Brian Mowry.
(Doug Loving)*

STARTING WITH A PUPPY

It is every Schutzhund trainer's dream to raise a dog from puppyhood through adulthood and achieve the highest levels of Schutzhund. As a master painter selects a blank canvas and paints, setting out to create a masterpiece, so it is with the handler who does all the training, from puppyhood on into adulthood.

This team's success will be a direct reflection of the training abilities of the handler. It is perhaps the most difficult task in Schutzhund, and it demands a high level of skill from the trainer. Even with the proper knowledge to get the job done, all kinds of problems can crop up. Some are simply not preventable with puppies. For example, health problems, hip or elbow dysplasia, early unavoidable trauma or some other unforeseen tragedy may prevent the dog from working out as planned.

A skilled trainer can select, with high proficiency, pups that will turn out to be successful Schutzhund candidates. But no one can claim to be 100 percent successful in these predictions; there are too many variables in genetic makeup and unforeseen factors that will affect the puppy in his first year of life.

The benefits of starting out with a puppy are:

- You can socialize the puppy to your environment. If you have children, pets or livestock, you can teach the puppy proper behavior around them from the start. This will help to ensure that the puppy will not become aggressive toward them later on.

- You can form the habits and manners you want in your puppy from the start.

- You can begin conditioning the dog to be confident with the things he will encounter later in training, such as training sticks (called *schlagstocks*), gunfire, jumps and dumbbells. You can also start the dog early in tracking.

- The dog is bonded to you, his handler, and learns to do what you want because he wants to please you as well as satisfy his own natural drives. This is probably the most important advantage.

- You will receive the most recognition from your peers, since this is the most difficult way to go about competition.

- This is the least expensive way to go.

Ivan Balabanov's Malinois, Nakita Des Deux Pottois, SchHIII, IPOIII, FH, with puppies. One of these puppies grew up to be the 1998 DVG Champion and another placed third the same year.

PICKING THE RIGHT PUPPY

Once you have decided to get a puppy and have chosen the breed, you are ready to select a breeder. Generally speaking, the best dogs for Schutzhund come from lines that have been worked in Schutzhund for many generations. These dogs have been selectively bred for generations to perpetuate the necessary drives in their offspring.

How well a dog grips is largely genetic. In the sport of Schutzhund, the fact that the dog can bite is not enough. The bite is judged very harshly. To get the highest points, the bite must be full (with the entire mouth) and hard, but at the same time calm. These traits can be largely genetic. However, one can improve—or ruin—the bite with training.

A Schutzhund prospect must be active in order to succeed and enjoy the sport. The sport requires a dog with good endurance, as there are many exercises that involve running and jumping. Excellent health and anatomical makeup are of critical importance to withstand the rigors of regular weekly training and intense physical competition. The dog must be free of hip and elbow dysplasia and other joint problems, and any inherited traits that could affect his freedom of movement and cause pain.

The dog's nerves are also very important. He should be calm and should not overreact to new stimuli. He should be social and neither aggressive nor fearful with strangers.

Our advice is to do a lot of research before buying your puppy. Study the breed, the breeder and the breeding your puppy will come from. It is hard enough to train an excellent dog for Schutzhund; forget about one that is lacking any of the criteria we've just mentioned.

When selecting a breeder, you may want to start by looking through Schutzhund or breed-specific magazines, or attending a Schutzhund trial. If you see a particular dog you like, seek out the owner and find out more about the lines the dog has descended from. Do this with a few dogs and you will get a good idea of the pros and cons of different lines and what you can expect from the breed you have chosen.

A word of caution: Try to confirm from a second source any rumors you might hear about a particular dog or line of dogs. As in any sport, you will run into some jealousy and malice. You may get incorrect information from a breeder with a private grudge against another breeder. Always try to find a second party who is not biased. If you are surfing the Internet for information on breeders, do not accept at face value everything you see advertised, either. Just because someone says they are the National Champion or have a certain title does not necessarily mean it's true!

When looking at the parents of your working puppy, don't neglect to watch the parents work. If you can't get to a competition in person, watching a videotape is fine. Just don't accept the stories of the owner. If one parent is a working dog and the other is from working lines, this could be fine, as long as the untrained dog didn't wash out in training (meaning he didn't possess the proper drives or abilities).

For example, if we have a bitch born from Schutzhund III parents, but we acquired her at three years of age from a couple who chose not to compete with her, this doesn't mean she should not be bred, nor does it mean she can't do the work. If you want to buy one of her puppies, you should expect that they have bred her to a top-working male. We could choose a Schutzhund III male, for instance, as the stud dog. You should also expect to see her and assess her temperament, obedience, tracking, protection work and whatever other training (personal protection, agility and so on) we can show you.

When shopping for a top-quality puppy, do not underestimate the importance of the bitch. She is, after all, 50 percent of the breeding. She is also the one that will raise the pups until weaning and, to a great degree, they will follow her lead.

Take into consideration what the breeder tells you about the pups. He or she has spent the most time with them during their development and can tell you a lot about them. The way puppies act will change according to their age and the time of day, and the puppies may act differently around you than they usually do. The breeder can tell you this. Weigh your observations with those of the breeder.

You want a puppy that is outgoing, likes to play, approaches when new stimulus is introduced, is curious and likes to use his mouth to play and explore. Avoid the hyperactive puppy or the one that shows shyness or a lack of desire to follow and play. Your puppy should appear healthy and happy, even when in a new environment. You must look at the puppy by himself, as well as with his litter mates.

Here is a quick checklist of things you should look for when purchasing a prospective Schutzhund puppy:

- Schutzhund or other working titles (KNPV, French Ring, DPO, and so on), sport or police titles on the parents and/or grandparents, to ensure selective breeding for working traits.

- Orthopedic Foundation for Animals (OFA) or PennHIP certification on the hips and elbows of the sire and dam.

- Any other health certification required in your particular breed, such as an eye test (CERF) or hearing test (BAAR).

- See the sire and dam and watch them work, whenever possible.

- See other offspring from either the sire or the dam, whenever possible. If this litter is a repeat breeding, see past offspring from the first litter, whenever possible. This will give you excellent information, as your puppy will most likely be very similar. *Never expect to get offspring better than the sire or dam.*

- Get references from the breeder and call them. Even if the references are biased in favor of the breeder, the fact that they can give you several references is a good sign.

- Talk to other Schutzhund enthusiasts about your decision. Keep an open mind, open ears and a closed mouth (best if you want to make new friends, not enemies).

As you can see, buying a puppy can be a lot of work and requires a great deal of research. There are both great rewards and great pitfalls possible with this choice.

PURCHASING A YOUNG, GREEN DOG

The benefit of purchasing a young dog with little or no training is that you can see what you are getting. You do not need a crystal ball to tell you what this dog will be like in a year. This is a very popular shortcut, rather than starting out with a puppy.

The possible drawback here is that you are going to get whatever was put into the dog before you bought him. Depending on who had the dog and what habits he learned, this could be good or bad.

For instance, if you live on a horse ranch and buy a 14-month-old German Shepherd that has never seen a horse, you may have a problem. Likewise, if the dog was exposed to someone who abused him at a young age, even though he is a great dog in every way, you may find that his courage has a limit because of his previous experiences.

Still, there are many benefits to purchasing a young, green dog:

- You can see what you are getting and know the dog's temperament is not likely to change much beyond this age. This means you can be fairly sure the dog will be capable of the work.
- While this dog may cost you two to three times more than a puppy, he will still cost less than a titled Schutzhund dog.
- You can see preliminary hip, elbow and back X-rays that can warn you if a problem is developing.
- The training will still primarily be yours. The dog has probably only had some preliminary puppy training, and is now just old enough to start serious training.

SELECTING A YOUNG DOG

If you want to jump ahead by a year and start your training with a dog that is ready to go, the young, green dog may be your best bet. Your primary reasons for starting with this dog will probably be to shorten the training process and to determine health and anatomical correctness.

Finding the proper dog may be difficult. If you have a certain breed and certain criteria in mind, it could take you months or even years to find the right dog. Good young dogs are in great demand. And they generally cost quite a bit more than a puppy.

Here is a checklist of important considerations when purchasing a young, inexperienced dog.

- Look for working lines. As with a puppy, see the parents and siblings, if possible.

- See for yourself the dog's drives and willingness to please. Have the dog looked at by another trainer or experienced club member if you need assistance.

- Have the dog checked by a veterinarian. Have X-rays taken of the dog's hips, back and elbows to ensure there are no problems developing.

- Ask the owner/seller of the dog if there are any quirks that they know of. Questions should include things that will be important to you. For instance, if the dog is extremely dog aggressive, you could end up working on eliminating this behavior for a long time. This could affect your ability to compete. Is the dog afraid of water? Aggressive to livestock? Afraid of slippery floors? Excessively defensive around strangers? An escape artist? Fence jumper? Cat chaser?

After you find a good prospect, you may have some hurdles to overcome because of the dog's previous upbringing. If the dog was kept in a kennel for the majority of his life, you may have to housebreak him. He may not be well socialized or may be overly aggressive, fearful of other dogs or afraid of slippery surfaces. Your individual lifestyle and desires will determine whether a particular dog will fit your needs. You must weigh all of the potential drawbacks against the potential gains to decide if the dog is right for you.

STARTING WITH AN ADULT TITLED DOG

This is a favorite way for novices to start in Schutzhund. Buying a titled dog and competing with him allows the handler to first learn about

Schutzhund from a handler's perspective, before learning how to actually train a dog. (Of course, a titled dog still needs training to maintain and polish his skills.) That's because handling a dog and training a dog are two entirely different things. As long as the dog has been worked in a particular exercise, the handler just needs to learn to signal the dog and properly command him.

Schutzhund-titled dogs can cost several thousand dollars. The cost will depend on the dog's points and breed worthiness (in other words, value as a stud or brood bitch). Be sure you deal with a reputable seller or importer when buying your dog. There are many horror stories out there from buyers who have been duped by unscrupulous sellers who knowingly sell dogs with existing hip, health or temperament problems.

The benefits of buying a titled adult are:

- Instant gratification. You have an adult, ready to go. You can go right out and practice, and can start competing soon.
- The dog will help teach you how to handle.
- You can watch the dog work, have your vet checks done and pretty much know what you have before you buy.
- You avoid the frustrations and setbacks that can come with training a dog.

CHOOSING A TITLED ADULT

If you decide to get a titled adult, you most likely are doing so because you want to jump right into the sport. Most people who go this route don't have the time or inclination to develop a young dog, or perhaps they lack the skill or knowledge to bring a young dog along.

Here is a checklist that you can follow when you're shopping for a titled adult dog:

- Confirm for yourself that the dog, whether foreign or domestic, really is titled. The dog should be tattooed or microchipped, and should have a scorebook and a certificate with the title and the dog's name.
- Make sure the dog comes with X-rays. Have your own vet examine the dog and take X-rays if there are questions or doubts. You always have the option to get new X-rays and compare the two.

• Work the dog, or have an experienced trainer work him, to make sure he has good potential to meet your needs.

The best years for a Schutzhund dog are from four to six. This is when the dog is at his peak of performance. If you were to buy a six-year-old dog, you would probably only be able to compete with him for another two years or so. You are best off with a dog that is three to four years old at the time of purchase.

Living With a Schutzhund Dog

There are many myths about living with a dog that is in Schutzhund training. Just because the dog is involved in a protection sport doesn't mean he should be isolated from the rest of the world.

Some dogs are sport dogs only. This means the dog works purely for the fun of it. This dog may not actually protect, even if the handler is in real danger. Other dogs are dual trained for realism in protection. This has the potential to be a drawback in the sport because it makes the

Martha Hoffman's Malinois Amok Ot Vitosha, SchHIII, IPOIII, with friends.

dog more suspicious and therefore less calm and predictable in his field exercises. Many handlers wait to convert their Schutzhund dogs to real protection work until after they are finished with competition.

HOUSING CONSIDERATIONS

The Schutzhund dog must be lively and full of energy and mischief if he's going to have the drives needed for the work. This is especially true for a puppy. You can expect a strong will and a need to chew and explore the world by using his mouth. Crates and dog runs are critically important with a Schutzhund dog to keep him out of trouble.

Some trainers keep their dogs outside in dog runs as a form of training. This is not to make the dog unfriendly, but rather to keep him from playing and interacting with other dogs and people who may give him unconditional attention. The reasoning behind this is that if the dog receives attention without working for it, his need to gain attention through work will be diminished. This is a widely used training technique. The energy built up through confinement can then be channeled into training.

Once the foundation for training is established (generally during the first year or two of the dog's life), the dog can then be in the house or out, as much as you like. By this time the dog should be relatively mature and should enjoy training more than just running around and playing with other dogs.

Schutzhund trainers differ in their philosophy at this point. Some will keep the dogs in confinement when they're not working with them. Others will allow the dogs to be real house dogs; these dogs are still able to compete at the top levels of the sport. Either method can be used with success.

THE IMPORTANCE OF SOCIALIZATION

Schutzhund is a sport that demands the dog be social. Trials are large, crowded events, and the dog will need to behave and be approachable by strangers. *The Schutzhund dog is in no way the image of the defensive guard dog with teeth gnashing at strangers.* This is a very important point for readers who are new to the sport. There are many uninformed members of the public who think otherwise because they have not taken the time to discover the truth.

Ivan Balabanov's Belgian Malinois Boril Ot Vitosha, SchHII, socializing at a coffee shop.

The Schutzhund dog should be well socialized with children and people of all ages and appearances. Schutzhund is a sport where overly aggressive, fearful, shy, unsocial or physically weak dogs will not make it to competition. A good handler will take full responsibility to make sure their dog is not any of these things.

CARE AND FEEDING

The Schutzhund prospect should be under the care of a veterinarian who is experienced with working dogs. Immunizations, regular check-ups and X-rays (to see how the joints and back are holding up) may be in order. X-rays should be taken yearly for young dogs, and every two to three years, or as necessary, for older dogs.

Schutzhund is a physically demanding sport, and your puppy or dog should be on a strict diet of food that supplies enough protein for the work, but not so much that it creates panosteitis in a growing dog.

(*Panosteitis* is lameness in young dogs caused by over-rapid bone growth.)

It is very important that a Schutzhund dog remain lean because of the amount of running and jumping required in the sport. An overweight dog will not have the endurance to compete at the top levels. Consult your veterinarian for specific diet recommendations based on your dog's breed and current age.

To sum up, it's important to remember the following when living with a Schutzhund dog:

- A Schutzhund dog is not *automatically* a personal protection dog. He needs conversion training or civil defense work before he can be considered a personal protection dog. This work may make Schutzhund training more difficult, as you are heightening the dog's suspicion level.

- Dog runs and crates are critical for the first year or two of the Schutzhund dog's life. They help prevent destruction of property with a dog or pup that is very mouth-oriented by nature. They will also lessen the chance that the dog could swallow a foreign body that might poison him or block his intestines.

- The Schutzhund dog needs to be well socialized with children and adults of all types and ages in order to prevent fear or aggression toward strangers.

- The Schutzhund dog should be seen regularly by a veterinarian. The dog should be on a correct diet for the amount of work he is doing.

chapter 3

How Dogs Learn

In order to be a successful dog trainer, you must have two-way communication with your dog. It is crucial to your success that you understand how dogs learn and also what the likely result will be of the actions you take and the environment you place the dog in.

Nature has programmed the dog to learn quickly what works and what doesn't, in order to preserve the species. For a dog it's as simple as *this works and brings reward and pleasure,* or *this doesn't work and brings pain or an unpleasant experience.*

However, we need to realize that dogs associate their actions with an immediate consequence. Unlike humans, dogs cannot reason that an action that took place earlier can result in a punishment now. For example, a dog left in the house chews a sofa cushion. The owner, upon returning home, spanks the dog and puts him outside as punishment. This is human logic. *We* can understand that we are being punished for doing wrong, even if the event took place an hour ago. The dog, however, cannot associate the spanking and banishment with the chewing he did hours ago—not even if the cushion is brandished in his face. The dog must be able to directly associate a reward or a bad experience with his actions. He will then quickly adapt. And it's not only about survival to the dog—he will also be driven by what gives him pleasure.

What Is Learning?

One of the best definitions of learning is *a change of behavior due to experience.* We use the word change, rather than acquisition, because learning doesn't always appear to involve acquiring some piece of knowledge, but does involve some sort of change. While all learning involves changes in behavior, not all changes involve learning. For example, fatigue, injury and maturation can change behavior, but these are not considered learning. Learning refers only to changes in behavior due to experience.

In order to develop training methods, you need to understand the theories behind how dogs learn—in other words, how dogs are conditioned. The two prevailing theories that describe the conditioning process for dogs are Pavlovian Conditioning (also known as Classical Conditioning) and Operant Conditioning.

PAVLOVIAN CONDITIONING

Pavlovian Conditioning describes a dog's reflexive responses to stimuli, and how they can be shaped. With this kind of conditioning, the dog learns to pair a particular event with a particular response. Put another way, he learns to predict what will happen in conjunction with a certain action or environment. Once the dog learns that the prediction he has made is correct, he will begin to anticipate. At this point, we have a predictable reaction to a cue, or stimulus.

Pavlovian Conditioning breaks stimuli into two types. The first type is an *unconditioned stimulus,* which elicits a natural reflex or unconditioned response. For example, when presented with food (an unconditioned stimulus), a dog salivates (an unconditioned response). Salivation is an unconditioned response from the dog.

The second type is a *conditioned stimulus,* which implies learning and produces a conditioned response. To condition the dog, the unconditioned response is paired with a conditioned stimulus to lead to a conditioned response. The classic example of a conditioned response is a dog that salivates *in anticipation* of food when a cue is given, such as a bell. The bell is a conditioned stimulus, and the salivation is a conditioned response. In order to create this conditioned response, each time food is presented the bell is also rung. Soon the dog equates the bell with food, and will salivate whenever he hears the bell.

OPERANT CONDITIONING

Operant Conditioning theory explains how voluntary behavior from the dog will teach him that his actions have consequences, either negative or positive. Operant Conditioning describes four methods that increase desirable behavior and decrease undesirable behavior.

The first two methods are reinforcers, and they can be negative or positive. With *positive reinforcement* the dog is rewarded for a behavior: sit = treat. With *negative reinforcement,* the dog's desired behaviors are reinforced by removing adverse outcomes: sit = no jerk on the leash.

The other two methods use negative and positive punishment. With *positive punishment,* an adverse consequence is associated with unwanted behavior: no sit = jerk on leash. With *negative punishment,* the reward or positive outcome is removed when the dog displays unwanted behavior: no sit = no treat.

We'll discuss the training applications of positive and negative reinforcement and punishment in Chapter 4. Meanwhile, this diagram should help you better understand the four methods used in Operant Conditioning, the terms used to describe them and their intended results.

Operant Conditioning

	...Is Given	... Is Taken Away
Something Good ...	Positive Reinforcement sit = treat *(increases response)*	Negative Punishment no sit = no treat *(decreases response)*
Something Bad ...	Positive Punishment no sit = jerk on leash *(decreases response)*	Negative Reinforcement sit = no jerk on leash *(increases response)*

When you're thinking about training methods and what kind of reinforcement or punishment is being used, it may help to ask yourself these questions:

1. What behavior was changed?
2. Was the frequency of the behavior increased or decreased?
3. What was the consequence to the dog?
4. Was the consequence something that was given to the dog or something that was taken away?

Timing Is Everything

The way the conditioned stimulus and unconditioned stimulus are paired is very important for learning to occur. Trainers call this timing. There are four ways unconditioned stimuli and conditioned stimuli can be paired. To explain them, we'll use a typical training scenario: Using the command "no," paired with a leash correction, to stop an undesired behavior. In order for this to happen, the command "no," which is the conditioned stimulus, has to signal to the dog that the unconditioned stimulus, in this case the leash correction, is coming.

One of the ways to pair the two is called *trace conditioning*. Here the conditioned stimulus begins and ends before the unconditioned stimulus is presented. In our example, the trainer says "no" and then gives a leash correction.

The second way is called *delayed conditioning*. Here the conditioned stimulus starts before the unconditioned stimulus is presented, and ends as soon as the unconditioned stimulus is presented. In other words, they slightly overlap but the conditioned stimulus is presented first. In our example, the trainer says "nooo" and gives a leash correction while he is still saying the word "no." With both trace conditioning and delayed conditioning, the dog will make the association quickly.

The third way to pair the stimuli is called simultaneous conditioning. Here the conditioned stimulus and the unconditioned stimulus begin and end at the exact same time. In our example, the trainer says "no" and gives the leash correction at the same time. The leash correction ends just as the trainer finishes saying the word "no." Here the command "no" will not serve as an indication of the coming correction.

The fourth way is called backwards conditioning. Here the trainer gives the leash correction first and then gives the command "no." When this happens, there is no reason for the dog to associate the command "no" with the leash correction, since he already got the correction and could not do anything to avoid it. As you might imagine, simultaneous conditioning and backwards conditioning do not really help the dog learn associations between conditioned and unconditioned stimuli.

Training Terms

In the science of training, you'll find many more terms interspersed into a training program. It is important to understand what these terms mean and what training methods they describe, as well as the potential benefits and drawbacks of each.

SINGLE EVENT LEARNING

As you might imagine, *single event learning* is learning as the result of one single event. Such an event has to make a very big impression on the dog, making repetition of the lesson unnecessary.

For example, a young dog that is unfamiliar with the stick is hit firmly with it during its introduction. The event makes such an impression that the dog refuses to bite anytime the stick is present. He may even refuse to bite at other times, or with the same decoy. The point is, you may not have intended to teach this lesson, but the dog has learned it nonetheless.

EXTINCTION OF BEHAVIOR

Extinction of behavior occurs when a behavior is no longer reinforced— it doesn't lead to a reward. As a result, the dog eventually stops the behavior.

For instance, if you take a toy onto the training field and offer it as a reward for a good obedience performance, the toy reinforces the precise behavior. If the toy is never again given on the field as a reinforcer, the precise performance of the dog may diminish because the behavior is not rewarded. This is true even if the toy is present. In fact, if it is not offered as a reward, the dog will most likely lose interest in the toy.

PROMPTING

Prompting occurs when a lesson is set up in such a way that a dog cannot make a mistake. For instance, when you use a chute to teach a dog to jump, he has no opportunity to go around the jump. The advantage here is that the dog can *only* learn the right way to take the jump—never the wrong way. Prompting is used to speed up learning and to eliminate confusion.

THE PREMACK PRINCIPLE

Another interesting concept that most dog trainers use subconsciously because it works (but few know the term for) is the *Premack Principle*, named after researcher David Premack. It states that high-frequency, preferred behavior can be used to reinforce low-frequency behavior. Access to the preferred behavior is contingent upon completing the low-frequency behavior.

The idea is that a preferred activity can be used to reinforce some less favored activity. For example, a dog likes to play with toys, even when he's by himself. That's a high-frequency activity. When we use playtime with toys to motivate a dog to work in obedience, it reinforces the obedience work, making it more enjoyable.

DISCRIMINATION TRAINING

Discrimination training is when the dog is allowed to find out for himself which behavior will lead to reward. He also has the option to explore a variety of solutions to try to solve the puzzle. Discrimination training is often very useful. Once the dog has figured out what behavior brings the reward, he will not be tempted by distractions as long as the setup is correct. Discrimination training also eliminates the possibility that the dog will be rewarded for inappropriate behaviors.

Motivation Techniques

Many training methods are based on using physical punishment techniques to correct undesired behaviors. This is called *positive punishment.* What makes Ivan's style of training different from other Schutzhund trainers is that he withholds the reward as a punishment. This minimizes the escape/avoidance type of training, and is referred to as *negative punishment.*

In training we like to give the dog the opportunity to choose and experiment with his actions and find out for himself which of his behaviors will lead to the reward. What the dog will soon realize is that executing the command we have given is the only way to get to the reward. What we end up with, then, is a dog who perceives commands as help, not as the typical, "Do what I say, or else."

The way to make reward-withholding training work is to create a dog that is highly motivated for something. In tracking he will crave the food rewards on the track; in obedience he will want to play with a toy; in protection he will want to bite. Only *after* the desire is there will the rules of the game be introduced. This is done gradually, through different setups where the rewards are withheld until correct responses are elicited from the dog during the exercises.

We are not saying we don't use any physical corrections. But when we do use a physical correction, it's far more meaningful to the dog than it would be to a dog that is constantly corrected by physical punishment to make him perform correctly. We firmly believe you do not need a lot of corrections, electric collars or long lines to train a dog to reliably perform any task. What you do need is to out-think the dog and find ways to control the environment—which can make the training more fulfilling and fun for both dog and trainer.

Motivation

Motivation is what makes the dog do what he does. When training a dog, it is critical to know what the dog will perceive as a reward for a behavior and what will effectively be a punishment. Every dog is different. Some have a strong food drive and others a strong play drive. What will motivate one dog may not motivate the next. A good trainer not only learns to recognize which drives are strongest and work with them, but also tries to develop the dog's other drives.

It is important to realize that when we step onto the training field, we are not asking the dog to do anything he doesn't already know how to do. He knows how to sit, run, jump, climb, lie down, bark and bite. All we are teaching him is to do these things on command. This is a conditioned response.

For example, we must teach a dog that only the correct sit carried out at the right time will bring a reward. There are several ways to teach him this. On the Schutzhund field, we want a dog that carries out the commands in a willing manner, without stress or avoidance. This should be accomplished on one command, without additional cues from the handler.

Corrections are used to curb undesirable behavior. Some dogs are highly sensitive to a specific type of correction, and others seem unaffected by it. The experienced trainer can judge the proper level of correction with a given dog and adjust the level as if he were adjusting the volume on a radio.

When training a dog, it is important to know not only the right motivators and correction techniques for your dog, but also how to balance the two properly so that you do not lose control or squelch the dog's drive to do the work. This is a delicate balancing act.

A good trainer always tries to strike a balance between positive and negative input. Obedience on command is not natural for a dog and is, in fact, inhibitory. Once you understand this, it is easy to see why a dog might shut down and refuse to do the work. This is called *avoidance*. If too much correction is applied to a dog without benefit of reward, you risk shutting the dog down, thereby putting him into avoidance.

For the dog to be reliable, you must know how to bring about the best performance in that particular dog. Therefore, the better you understand how to communicate with your dog, the better you will be as a trainer at getting the most out of each dog.

Positive Reinforcers

Positive reinforcement is essential in training. The motivator or reinforcement (a toy, ball, game, food or whatever) has to be something the dog (not necessarily the trainer) likes. In addition, the timing of the reward is critical, so that it will reinforce the correct action. The dog must perceive that the motivator is being given as a reward, and understand exactly which behavior led to the reward.

VERBAL PRAISE AS A SECONDARY REINFORCER

The handler always has the ability to verbally praise the dog. This is the most basic type of motivation (although it is considered a secondary reinforcer and will be most effective if paired with a primary reinforcer such as food or a toy). A good working dog will always find his handler's praise and attention to be a motivator. If a dog does not find this attention motivating, you must ask yourself the question, "Is this dog the right dog for the task?" A true working dog will be motivated to please his handler as well as himself.

In addition, in order for the praise to reinforce a behavior, the dog must be seeking attention from his handler. You should work hard to make sure this is the case because in competition verbal praise is the only reinforcer that is allowed!

The inflection you use is also important and should change depending on the dog and the situation. Sometimes a calm, soft tone of voice is better than vigorous, loud praise, and the opposite is true in other situations. Some dogs become distracted by loud praise, while others need it to get their drives going.

FOOD

Food is what trainers call a *primary reinforcer.* This means the reinforcer satisfies the dog's biological urge for survival. Using food in training is an extremely valuable reinforcer that speeds up the learning process and also maintains the behaviors that have already been learned.

Scientific studies have shown that constant food rewards help to teach new behaviors, while food rewards used intermittently produce the best results from a dog after the behavior is well established. The intermittent rewards should be delivered on an unpredictable schedule because if the dog doesn't know when the food will be given, he will actually work harder.

Typically, when you're using food as a reward, you should use something more special than the dog's daily ration. This will tremendously increase the dog's desire to work. In our training we also like to vary the food rewards. Not knowing what kind of reward he will get keeps the dog even more interested in the reward.

It is a fairly common practice to withhold food from a dog before a training session. This, of course, motivates the dog to an even higher degree.

TOYS AND GAMES

As with food rewards, the ball, a game of tug and a toy are all primary reinforcers. While they are not necessary for a dog's survival, they tap into drives that are. A good Schutzhund prospect should have natural play and prey drives, and these drives are satisfied by toys and games.

If the dog lacks these drives, it is very important to work on developing them. But the play and prey drives cannot be developed by force; in fact, excessive force is more likely to result in avoidance. Dogs that lack these drives simply may not be right for Schutzhund.

Some dogs will perform better with food reinforcers and some will do better when reinforced with a toy. Generally speaking, food is used to teach a new behavior and toys are used when you want to improve the speed of an already learned behavior—but again, this varies from dog to dog. You should be able to recognize which reinforcer works best for this dog and in what situations.

THE HANDLER'S BODY LANGUAGE

A dog can only be as good as his handler. A handler needs to be willing to run, to act happy and excited and to motivate the dog if they expect their dog to run and be motivated. Dogs pay very close attention to our body language, and rely on it for important cues. Schutzhund places athletic demands on the handler as well as the dog.

Negative Reinforcement and Positive Punishment

It is not uncommon for dog trainers to confuse the concepts of *negative reinforcement* and *positive punishment*. Although they are closely related, they are not the same. With positive punishment, some aversive event takes places. An example is a leash correction given to a dog when he refuses to come on a recall. The dog is punished for not coming, so that in the future he will understand that if he doesn't come he will be corrected. Once the dog understands this, he will avoid the correction by coming to you. The absence of the correction is an example of negative reinforcement.

The key difference between the two concepts is that negative reinforcement will *reinforce* a behavior, while positive punishment will *stop* a behavior. We will be using the term *correction* to refer to positive punishment.

A dog may respond to positive punishment in one of four ways, depending upon the level of punishment and the temperament of the dog. It may:

1. Submit and avoid the correction by obeying the command
2. Flee
3. Fight
4. Freeze

Positive punishment is the method most commonly used to stop an undesired behavior. It does work when used properly, but you need to know what types of corrections are effective without being abusive. The obvious drawbacks to using positive punishment are obviously its very undesirable side effects: escape behaviors, aggression, apathy and quite often a generalized suppression of the behavior being punished. In other words, if a dog is punished for sitting in one situation, he may not sit in any situation.

A variety of corrections—types of positive punishment—are used in dog training. As with motivation, the necessary level of correction will vary from dog to dog. There is, however, a vast difference between correction and abuse, and it's a difference dog trainers must be aware of.

Besides the obvious moral and ethical problems arising from abuse, all trainers should realize that abuse only serves to squelch the spirit of the animal. With a diminished spirit, the dog cannot give a spirit-filled performance on the training field or in competition. To the novice enthusiast, the dog may appear to be performing the tasks to an acceptable level of adequacy. However, to the experienced eye, the dog will seem intimidated by the handler and excessively careful, and will lack the twinkle in his eye and the bounce in his step that are the hallmarks of winners.

Because the distinction between correction and abuse is so important, it's useful to define some terms. These definitions come right out of the dictionary.

- Correction: The act of correcting, an emendation, rectification, adjustment, rebuke or discipline.
- Compulsion: The act of compelling; to drive or urge forcefully or irresistibly. To cause to occur by overwhelming pressure.
- Force: The capacity for exerting strength, power, might, to coerce, persuade or convince. Compel by physical, mental or moral means.
- Abuse: To misapply, do wrong, injure, violate and defile.
- Torture: The act of willfully inflicting severe pain.

One other important point to remember about corrections: *Corrections should be used only when it has been proven that the dog knows what you are asking from him.* Correcting a dog for something he didn't understand in the first place falls under the definition of abuse.

USING POSITIVE PUNISHMENT

For a correction to be effective, it must be:

1. Immediate
2. Strong enough to suppress the unwanted behavior
3. Associated only with the unwanted behavior
4. Happen every time the unwanted behavior occurs

If you find yourself nagging a dog to do something several times in a short period, it's an indication that you need to alter your training. Continuing to repeat the same training and then nagging will get you nowhere. Instead, break the training into small, positive steps and chain them together later. This is more likely to get you back on track.

NEGATIVE PUNISHMENT: WITHHOLDING A REWARD

When the dog cares about a reward and will do anything to get it, withholding it can be an effective training correction. Withdrawal of an expected reward is a form of punishment that creates frustration in the dog. He is not working through escape-avoidance response, and therefore he will not need to flee, freeze or fight. Rather, he will keep trying to find the correct way to get his reward. If a dog is conditioned to play with a toy that he likes as a reward for completing a command or series of commands, he has already learned that by following the rules he gets the reward. When the dog doesn't follow the rules, he'll learn the result is no reward. Not getting that reward will make him focus on figuring out the rules.

This method gives the dog the option not to obey the command, and the opportunity to self-correct. Consider that the opposite of a reward is not physical punishment, but rather withholding a reward.

TIME OUT

Time outs work in much the same way as withholding the reward. If the dog is over-stimulated or overly distracted by other stimuli, rather than fighting him, a better tactic is to isolate him for 10 minutes away from the field and then try again. Don't isolate him for a long period of time, such as an hour or two, because the dog has a short attention span and may begin to entertain himself. This makes the correction less effective. If the dog is made to wait only 10 minutes or so, he may return to the field with an entirely different attitude.

Need we add that you must first determine that the dog does not wish to rest? If he does, a time out will not be a correction.

AVERSIVE TOOLS

Aversive tools are used to eliminate an undesired behavior by associating it with discomfort. For these tools to work, the correction must be timed so that the dog associates the undesired behavior with his action, and it must be powerful enough to eliminate the attraction of the behavior. You should always use the minimum amount of force necessary for the dog to mind the correction.

The most common aversion tool is a stern command "no!," coupled with a quick jerk and release of the training collar (standard choke or pinch collar). Other examples are water or lemon juice sprayed in the dog's face, a throw chain or an electronic collar.

You should realize that the use of pinch collars and electronic collars is *banned* from Schutzhund training. If you are found to be using one of these devices in practice before a trial, you can be disqualified. Having said that, it is a known fact that these devices are used in Schutzhund training and before trials all the time. We feel it is best to talk about this openly rather than to hide the fact. This way, we hope to help people understand how these devices work.

Let us begin by stating that we *do not* condone the use of the electronic collar as an integral part of any training method. The humane issues are important, but there is also another important consideration: An electronic collar is not the most effective long-term training method. At the same time, we acknowledge that it is used quite frequently because it works. We are *against* teaching exercises using an electronic collar. However, if it is used, it should only be used as a correction tool after a behavior has been learned.

For example, if we are protection training the dog and the dog does not yet understand that "out" means come off the sleeve, or if he doesn't feel comfortable letting go for fear he may be struck again, this is the wrong time to use the electronic collar. That's because shock is a form of punishment, but before we can punish a behavior, *we must be sure the dog already knows how to respond correctly* to the given command without distraction or stress. If he doesn't, the punishment is ineffective and abusive.

Consider the following laboratory experiment: A dog is placed in a large box that has two compartments. One compartment is insulated; the other is not, and can deliver an electric shock to the dog. The dog freely walks around both compartments. Then a light comes on and if the dog is in the noninsulated compartment, he receives a shock. Because of the shock, he moves around and eventually finds out that the shock is not present in the other compartment. After a few trials, when the light comes on the dog avoids the shock by quickly moving to the insulated side. He soon learns that the light is the cue to move to the insulated side of the box. As soon as the light goes off, he continues his normal behavior of walking on both sides, confident that he knows how to avoid the shock.

However, life is not a laboratory. In dog training, the dog will have many more options. This is why we believe electric impulse correction should only be used when we are sure the dog knows what is expected of him. This way, the shock is less confusing and more of a punishment for defiance, rather than a basic correction.

One thing we should acknowledge right away is that when an electronic collar is used and the dog is still reluctant to change his behavior, the handler should use caution when deciding what to do next. Although a stronger stimulus may work on the dog, it also escalates the pain! This is when it becomes an ethical issue of humane versus inhumane treatment of the animal. Nobody should ever step over this line just for the sake of sport.

The electronic collar has come a long way in its development. The options range from collars that give a warning buzz before correction to collars that offer various levels of stimulation, at the handler's discretion. As with all other forms of correction, selecting the level that will be successful comes down to the handler's judgement and experience. This is why *only* the most experienced trainers should use this method.

When using the electronic collar, the handler must adjust the proper level of stimulation for his or her dog. This is best done during an obedience exercise that a dog understands very well. This way, when a correction is given, there is no confusion. The handler must be aware of how much is too much and how much is too little. Be very aware that if you accidentally shock the dog at the wrong time, you can cause your training to backslide dramatically. This is another reason why electronic collars should only be used by experienced trainers.

We should never forget that not all dogs are right for Schutzhund. Some may be happier doing something else, and shocking them into a behavior that does not come naturally to them is abuse. No trainer should tolerate abuse. This is where the lines become blurred. Using an electric collar on a dog that has a low pain threshold or weak nerves is abuse. Using the same collar on a bold dog with a high pain threshold is not. The same can be said for pinch collars.

If you are going to use an electronic collar (and remember, we do not believe it is necessary), use it carefully and humanely. The best results will be achieved if you put the collar on two hours before training and take it off an hour after. This way, the dog will not associate it as strongly with the training.

An important advantage of electronic collars is that they enable the handler to correct the dog from a distance and without a leash. Probably the best situation in which to turn to this method is when every other training solution has been tried and the dog is a tough animal with a high pain threshold. Even then, the collar should only be used as an aid and should never be relied upon as the sole means of training.

The downside of using electronic collars to solve problems is that they allow the handler to be lazy. The handler may not bother to figure out why a dog is behaving a certain way and may not try to solve the problem by using psychology—which is much longer lasting and better for the dog.

In another behavioral experiment, a dog was placed in a shuttle box that had a barrier between two compartments so that the dog could not move from one to the other. He was exposed to random shocks that he could not avoid no matter what he tried: whining, barking, jumping, etc. After awhile the dog simply laid down and accepted the shock. This is called *learned helplessness*. Once the dog knew he could not avoid the shock, the barrier was removed and the dog had the option to move to the other side of the box to avoid it, but he did not. This experiment was done with a large number of dogs, and results were always the same.

Next, the experimenters moved the dog to the other side of the box to show him that there was a way to avoid the shock. Most dogs did not respond to this, and the very few that did needed more than 200 tries to learn the behavior.

Yet another disadvantage of using electronic collars is that some dogs become "collar wise." This means the dog will obey 100 percent when the collar is on, but will be as unruly as ever when it is taken off. This occurs most often when the handler becomes lazy and "collar happy," using the electronic collar for every type of correction.

We prefer to use negative punishment (withholding the reward) as a first step—and most of the time the only step—in stopping an undesired behavior, rather than using electronic collars or other forms of force training. This allows the dog to learn by himself that he has to follow the rules in order to get what he wants. This involves no collars, no cheating and no physical punishment. It is up to him to learn from his own mistakes. In a trial the dog will be more comfortable and more honest in his performance than he would be after force training. This is because the dog has learned how to *think* about his own actions, and *not just react.*

COMPULSION

To be able to read a dog well enough to use compulsion successfully takes some experience. The correction has to be strong enough to block the distraction—but no more and no less. You must also be able to bring the dog into high drive immediately after the correction, if needed. Severe corrections don't help.

Always important in training, but especially when using compulsion, is to have something the dog really wants from you. If you don't have anything that motivates the dog, your training results may decline, or the dog will perform solely out of avoidance.

Having given you all these warnings, here is an example of a compulsion technique that may be helpful in *some* situations where *everything else* has failed. With this technique, you use a strong physical correction immediately after giving the command, but *before* the dog has a chance to do anything. This might entail pulling up on the collar for a sit, or down on the collar for a down. The idea is to motivate the dog to beat the correction with his response (an example of Classical Pavlovian Conditioning).

The level of correction must be judged very carefully, according to the individual dog. You want the dog to become reliable, not to panic or shut down. And this is not an ongoing method. The compulsion shouldn't become the cue for your command!

Keep in mind that the effect of compulsion techniques—improving the behavior or making it worse—usually doesn't show up in the same session, but in the following one. This is because the compulsion creates avoidance behavior, as well. Hopefully, in the next session the dog will show more correct behavior and less avoidance, and not the opposite. The best thing to do is wait and see how he does during the next session, instead of trying to make it perfect today.

The Schutzhund III Tracking Test

Tracking is undoubtedly the hardest phase of Schutzhund for most trainers. Even if you own an excellent tracking dog, there will be worries about the conditions of the track and how the dog will perform that day. This is especially true in important trials at the top levels of the sport. Like the Olympics, sometimes things just boil down to the luck of the draw.

Tracking is different from obedience and protection exercises in that the dog must perform at the trial without additional commands. In obedience or protection, you periodically give the dog commands that stimulate responses. In tracking, there is only the initial command to track. After that, you must simply trust the dog.

Let's begin by taking a look at the rules for the tracking test and what the judges are looking for when they score. (The rules for the track layer, the handler and the dog are adapted from the *United Schutzhund Clubs of America Official Rule Book*.)

The Track

- The track is 800 to 1,000 paces long.
- The subject is a stranger.
- The track is 50 minutes old.
- Three articles are left on the track.
- The track will have four 90° right-angle turns.
- The judge will determine the course of the track, taking into consideration the existing terrain.
- Whenever possible, tracks should be different shapes. Care should be taken to place articles at different points on the track. Corners should occur at different points from one trial to another.
- The start of the track should be visibly marked with a flag, sign or marker that will be pressed into the ground on the left side of the starting point.

The Track Layer

- The track layer should proceed to the starting point and remain there for some time.
- The track layer will then proceed *as indicated by the judge* and will place the first article after approximately 100 paces.
- The track layer must show the articles to the judge before laying the track.
- The track layer will use articles that are practical, carry the scent of the track layer, are no bigger than a wallet and do not differ in color from the terrain. Eyeglass cases, wallets, etc., can be used.
- The articles must be placed *on* the track, not next to it.
- The second article will be deposited on the middle of the second *or* third leg. This will be done without interrupting pace or changing stride.
- The third article will be deposited at the end of the track.
- The track layer will then proceed a few steps straight ahead and then move away from the track.

Typical Schutzhund III Track

250-300 paces

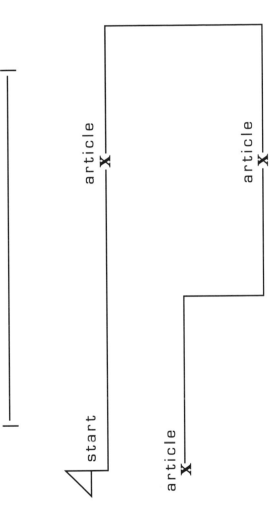

The Handler

- The handler has the option of tracking with the dog on a 10-meter leash or freely off leash. Both methods will be scored identically.
- While the track is being laid, the dog and handler will be out of sight.
- The handler will prepare the dog for the exercise and report to the judge when called upon.
- The handler will advise the judge whether the dog will pick up or indicate (point out) the article. To do *both* is faulty.
- Before and during tracking, the handler must not correct or coerce the dog in any way.
- The handler should allow the dog to absorb the scent for sufficient time at the start of the track. The handler should not allow the dog to be impetuous.
- The handler must follow the dog at a distance of 10 meters, with or without a leash.
- The tracking leash may be held loosely by the handler.
- When the dog indicates a find, the handler should drop the leash and proceed immediately to the dog. The handler should then pick up the article indicated and show it to the judge by lifting it high in the air. It is permissible for the dog to pick up the article as the handler steps toward him, as long as it is released immediately.
- After completing the track, the handler will hand the articles to the judge.

The Dog

- When directed by the judge, the dog should be led quietly and slowly to the starting point. The dog should be placed at the start of the track.
- The dog must quietly pick up the scent with a deep nose.
- The dog should move forward as the line plays out to a distance of 10 meters in the handler's hands. Whether on or off leash,

Kelly Martin's A'Shane Ot Vitosha, SchHIII, IPOIII, taking High in Tracking with 100 points at the 1997 DVG Nationals. (Nanette Nickherson)

the handler must not follow until the 10-meter distance is reached.

- Immediately after the dog has found the article, he must pick it up or indicate clearly through stopping and standing, sitting, lying down or returning to the handler. Forward motion while holding the article or picking it up while lying down is faulty.

Scoring

Scoring is calculated based on 100 possible points. The following are deductions for tracking faults.

Four-Point Deductions

- A faulty start
- Trailing

- Excessive circling on corners
- Continued praise
- Faulty picking up and dropping of articles
- Faulty pointing out of articles
- Faulty article detection
- Indication of false articles

Seven-Point Deductions

- Dog does not indicate an article

Eight-Point Deductions

- Repeated starts and pronounced trailing
- Tracking with a consistently high nose
- Impetuous tracking
- Urinating or defecating on the track
- Chasing animals (mice, birds, etc.) or insects

MORE ON SCORING

There are some other fine points of scoring that must be considered when you're tracking with a dog. Before starting the track, you are not allowed to do any obedience control work with the dog within six feet of the starting point—the scent pad. The judge wants to see that the dog is tracking freely and isn't being forced to work.

Upon reaching the starting area, you can either walk the dog up to the scent pad or begin tracking before the scent pad by giving the command to track. This is the handler's choice.

After issuing the command, you must stand still and feed the line out as the dog goes down the track. Only when you reach the end of the tracking line should you move forward. The same applies after each article has been indicated. In addition, you must hold the line with consistent tension, or points will be deducted for inconsistency.

You are allowed to point at the track only once, at the beginning when the initial command to track is given. After this, another hand signal will result in a point deduction. Every hand signal is considered to be a restart, which takes eight points off your score, so you must always make sure the signal is absolutely necessary—in other words, the dog will fail the exercise if you don't point. This is especially true *after* an article indication.

Overshooting corners may not be considered faulty if it is due to the prevailing wind conditions. If the direction of the wind carries the scent past the corners, overshooting may be a natural consequence.

Equipment Used in Tracking

Tracking equipment can vary quite a bit. Some dogs track with a line attached to the "dead ring" of a fur-saver collar, and some on a harness. In all big trials, expect your equipment to be checked by the judge. Dogs will not be allowed to track on leather or pinch collars.

Your tracking line *must* be 10 meters long. If you try to use a longer line but mark it and hold it at 10 meters, you will still lose points.

You should try different types of equipment to determine what is most comfortable for you and your dog. You may even find that different equipment works better under different conditions. Always keep in mind the weather that you may be tracking in.

What the Judge Wants to See

First and foremost, the judge wants to see the *desire* and ability of the dog to track. The dog should not appear careless or look pressured or stressed while working. Speed is also important. A good judge will not deduct points from a dog for tracking too fast, unless this creates mistakes or sloppiness. But a fast-tracking dog, in most cases, tends to overshoot the corners, miss articles and may show some hectic circling behaviors when faced with a problem, such as a change of weather or terrain. Such a dog is a very eager tracker and will usually not quit on the track, although he will lose points for his mistakes.

The extremely slow tracking dog, on the other hand, does not show enough commitment. This dog is much more likely to quit on a track when faced with problems. The slow tracker will typically receive an excellent score on a familiar course or under easy conditions, such as familiar weather and terrain, but may quit at the very beginning of a difficult track.

A methodical tracker falls between the two ends of the spectrum, being neither slow nor fast. This is a balanced dog. He is most likely a good problem solver, not losing his patience or desire to track when he encounters a problem. This dog should stay focused and work at a consistent speed. Most important, he should show the ability to work independently on *any* track and in *any* weather conditions.

While the judge should not deduct points from a fast or slow tracker, the judge *will* deduct points if the tracking speed is inconsistent or choppy. Make sure your dog sets a pace that he can maintain for the length of the track.

Tracking Psychology

There are no shortcuts to tracking at the highest levels of competition. It takes a lot of time and effort from both trainer and dog to achieve a high level of performance at the trial. *Most successful trainers will track every day for at least 10 days before going to trial!* Consider it pure luck if you track once a week and then get a good score on trial day.

Ivan Balabanov's Django Ot Vitosha at six months old is at the starting point for a practice puppy track. (Carolyn Niehaus)

An individual training program for tracking should be designed to fit each dog's temperament. With some dogs, it is beneficial to work two to three tracks a day. Others do best when working only one track, four times a week. Even this routine may need to be changed when working on particular problems. For example, if your goal is to work on article indication, there is no need to lay one really long track with a few articles. It would be better to lay a few short tracks with more articles. Doing this will emphasize the articles to the dog, and you will also benefit by being able to take short breaks in between tracks.

The Importance of Weather and Terrain

It is extremely important during tracking training and competition to take notes about the track. Note the age and length, how many left and right turns, the weather when the track is laid, the weather when the course is tracked, cross-tracks and so on. These notes will help you understand where your dog has difficulties and what weather and terrain conditions can cause problems.

If you don't take notes, you may be confused by the dog's responses and not see the pattern of problems. When you know why your dog is having difficulties, you can design a training program that concentrates on the problem areas. But when all you know is that things are going wrong, there's not much you can do to fix them. The dog should not be able to predict the track. The handler, on the other hand, should know every turn and the difficulty level for the dog in question.

Problem Solving in Advanced Tracking

Many of the problems in tracking come about because tracking requires so much trust between dog and handler. On the day of a trial, you will not know where the track goes, and must trust your dog to follow it faithfully. But unless you have already trained your dog to solve problems on his own, he will be looking to you for clues that you can't give.

Tracking Too Fast

The dog that tracks too fast is generally motivated to get to the end of the track and gain a reward. If the reward is food and the dog is hungry, the desire for food may be so great that the dog rushes through the track, missing dropped articles or turns. If a toy is the reward, the drive to get it may ultimately cause the same mistakes.

With both the food and the toy, you have made the end point the most important goal for the dog. It does not take long for the dog to realize this and to figure out that the goal is to get to the end of the track as fast as possible.

There are many ways to keep the dog focused on the entire track, instead of just the end point. If you are sure the problems you are experiencing are caused by the food or toy reward at the end of the track, you may want to eliminate the final reward altogether and simply offer more food on the track. This lowers the motivation for the fast tracker to get to the end, but since the dog already enjoys the process of tracking, he will still continue to track for you. Finish the track with an article, and then take the dog off the track before you reward him with treats.

The next time you track, you may want to reward at the second article, and calmly take the dog off the track at the end and reward him with calm praise. This way, you keep the dog from generalizing where the rewards will be. He learns that he must work carefully on the entire track if he is to find the rewards and be successful. You may also experiment with what time you feed the dog the night before, or even try feeding him right before tracking. Try this several times before deciding if the new schedule works, as it takes a while to break an established behavior pattern.

Another method is to reward the dog at several points on the track, possibly with handfuls of food whenever an article is found. This establishes gratification *within* the track. You can also intermittently reward the dog with small tidbits along the track on an unpredictable schedule. This will hold the dog's attention on the track itself, rather than focusing him on the end of the track.

Speed is also encouraged when too much emphasis is placed on weaning the dog from food on the track. A handler will typically put less food on the first leg of the track and more at the end. If you stay at this level for long, the dog will learn to rush to where the food is. Ideally, the dog should *never* be able to anticipate where on the track he will find rewards.

If the dog's reward is a toy because he is motivated to play, a similar strategy would be to play with him *before* tracking. Many trainers are reluctant to do this because they think the dog's drive to go down the track will be diminished when he already has the satisfaction of playing. The key is to put the toy away after playing for 10 or 15 minutes, and give the dog a break and some water. Then take the dog out and work the track.

THE PRETENDER

Another reason a dog might track too fast is that he feels pressured by the handler. Some handlers nag their dogs, expecting perfection, and signal the dog by giving small jerks on the leash. This only confuses the dog and turns up the pressure. The dog may anticipate a turn or lie down on an imaginary article. The dog may also move along too quickly, thinking this is what you want. This dog is *pretending* to know what he's doing because he figures this is the way to avoid your correction.

A dog can easily learn to do this if he is hurried along when he comes to an interesting object on the track. For instance, if a piece of paper is next to the track and the dog is hurried past it rather than being allowed to check it out, the dog may be receiving the message that continued forward motion is more important than being thorough.

When a dog first learns to track, it's a good idea to let the dog check out the footsteps of someone who crossed the track, as well as the odd rock or small piece of paper on the track, so that he will understand these are not articles to find. This does not mean the dog should be allowed to wander a few feet off the track in order to check things out. A balance should be struck.

Unfortunately, most handlers will rush in toward the dog the minute they notice him checking out something that the human knows is insignificant. The problem is *the dog* doesn't know the item is insignificant. He just thinks he's being prodded to track faster. As the dog becomes more proficient at tracking, you can slowly begin to minimize the amount of time the dog spends checking out stray items and scents on the track.

It is also important not to make a habit of running up to check out what is on the track when the dog pauses to sniff something. The dog is likely to think he's about to be corrected, and may be tempted to move on without satisfying his curiosity. You have unintentionally pushed the dog into going faster. This, in turn, causes missed turns and unfound articles. You should slow down and give the dog time to satisfy his curiosity and decide to move on.

It also helps if you walk slowly up to the dog from time to time and, in a calm and soothing manner, verbally and physically praise him. This reassures him that he will be allowed the time to finish the food reward or to check the article on the track.

The key, from the handler's point of view, is to know when your dog is *working* and when he is *getting off task*. This is one reason why it is so important to really know your dog. There are subtle changes in body language when a dog changes intention. This body language may be so slight that it is easily missed by someone less in tune with the dog.

Carolyn Niehaus reassures C'Ivanna Ot Vitosha, SchHI, while tracking under difficult conditions.

Other kinds of stress can also push the dog to work too fast. The collar, obviously, has a great effect on the dog's comfort and stress levels in tracking. Using a harness, flat collar or fur-saver instead of a pinch collar, for instance, makes the dog less concerned about avoiding a correction.

Your intent in tracking should always be to impress upon your dog that he can work *without* your help or correction. After all, this is the way your dog *must* work in competition. Don't be afraid to go back to the beginning at any time. Working on the simple stuff builds confidence and helps to maintain calmness in the dog.

The dog that tracks too fast will often be overly excited to continue on the track once he has lain down next to (or indicated) the article. It can sometimes be better to keep the dog in a down for a moment or two in order to relax him and lessen the stress of tracking. However, if this does not work with your dog, never force it. Forcing a dog to hold the down will only create more stress. The idea is to relieve stress, and what relieves stress is different for every dog.

DESTINATION ORIENTATION

Psychologically, it is a good idea to teach your dog that a track does not always go off into the distance. To do this, you can make a four-by-four-foot scent pad and really kick in the scent, and then push some food into the ground at the spot so that the dog must use his paws or nose to retrieve it. You may also want to lay a track in a triangle or a square, which brings the dog back to the starting point. This teaches the dog that the track doesn't always go somewhere far away, thereby slowing him down naturally.

Another useful exercise for this problem is tracking on surfaces that are less stable. A deeply plowed field with big clods of dirt, or a wet surface where the dog sinks a little, will slow him naturally.

Tracking *with* the wind should be a priority for quite some time. This is done so that the dog does not pick up the scent in advance—which encourages fast tracking. You will ultimately have to track under all four wind directions, but do use the wind to your advantage when you're working on a problem. When you track against the wind, you will want to make short legs (sections of track) to help slow the dog down.

You can also slow the dog by having him track footprint by footprint. Have your track layer leave wide spaces between footprints in a straight line, and place plenty of food on the track. Gradually move the footprints closer together, back to a normal pace, as the dog learns to track at a more suitable speed.

When tracking in ideal conditions where footsteps are visible to a dog, cross-tracks may be helpful in slowing him down. Using someone else's cross-track forces the dog to focus more and use his nose. In order for the dog to stay on the track, he must slow down.

SOME BASIC GUIDELINES

Every tracking training session should be well thought out beforehand so that it is a new experience for your dog. The dog should not be able to predict how long the track will be, what the articles will be or where he will find rewards. It is important to set up a scenario where the dog can achieve his goal, while at the same time keeping the difficulty level high enough to maintain his interest.

When a dog tracks too fast, it is important to track as often as possible. Daily would be best because this keeps the excitement level even and makes for more steady, consistent work. Keep the tracks short. There is a big misconception that long tracks will slow a dog down, but this is never really the case. Although the dog may tire and eventually slow toward the end of the track, the next time a track is started, he will track just as fast.

As the dog's speed becomes steadier and he is working every corner nicely and indicating every article, don't slow the dog down more than you need to   even if he still goes faster than other dogs. Dogs, like people, are individuals. You have to observe your particular dog's personality. Slowing down some dogs can be difficult, if not impossible—and why would you want to if the dog is tracking well?

Quitting on the Track

There are several reasons why a dog might quit on a track, but the most common is a lack of motivation. Rushing to wean the dog from his food or toy reward and making the tracking too formal or difficult reduces the dog's motivation. The dog must always have enough rewards on the track to create the desire to work. Weaning should be a gradual process.

Using compulsion when the dog lacks motivation is the worst thing you can do because compulsion will never restore a dog's desire to work. Correction should be used only as a reminder to go and look for the reward. The dog should not get the impression that you are forcing him to go forward, even though there is no reward. Remember, it is the *impression* you give the dog that will either squelch his drives or motivate him.

PUZZLING THROUGH PROBLEMS

A dog may also quit on a track because he doesn't know how to solve a problem. This is especially true if you rush in to try to force the dog to do something. Instead of forcing the dog, you need to take a step back. Introduce the same problem again, but this time make it easier for the dog to solve. This will build the dog's confidence.

For instance, if you are having difficulties with a change of terrain, have the dog cross over just four feet of grass instead of an entire field, or a small ditch or puddle rather than a larger stream. Let the dog *learn how* to solve these kinds of problems before you expect him to work out great distances or big problems. Gradual and systematic training is the key.

BREAKING THE CYCLE OF COMPULSION

If your dog has been quitting on the track, and serious compulsion has been applied without the desired effect, step back. Give the dog a break from training for a week or two. After the break, try to change everything that your dog associates with compulsion, including:

- The field you're tracking on
- The terrain you're tracking on
- The collar on the dog
- The rewards used
- The frequency with which rewards are found
- The distance between the dog and handler
- Anything else that may have an association in the dog's mind with compulsion

Try to change your routine, as well. For example, you might add something new, such as having the dog sit before the tracking command is given. This is all done to put him at ease. Your goal is to show the dog that everything has changed, and you will now allow him to track without using force.

At this point, make a short track (maybe 50 paces) over terrain the dog is comfortable tracking on. Let the dog work the track at his own pace, and reward him as much as possible with things like extra food, praise or a little play session on the tracking field. This is all done so the dog will perceive the tracking field as the best place to be. When the track is completed, stop for the day. Don't do more than one track.

To build excitement for tracking, track only once or twice a week and make sure the dog is bored at home. That means no play or exercise sessions except on the track. Your goal is to change your dog's attitude toward tracking, so tracking should be the outlet for his pent-up energy.

Stick to this program until you see the dog's enjoyment of tracking increase (it could take a while). Then you can move on toward your next goal.

Medical and Environmental Problems

Sometimes what appears to be a training problem is really a medical or environmental problem. It is your responsibility to rule out these problems. Medical problems, such as ear infections, can irritate a dog and cause him to quit on the track. And anything that causes pain while working, such as arthritis, can obviously make tracking difficult. In this case, you should be taking the dog to the vet rather than trying to change his attitude.

Learn about particular grasses and which ones give off strong scents or might contain irritating seeds or burrs. Foxtails and freshly sprayed fields are other potential problems to be aware of. Find out which areas may have insects such as spiders or yellow jackets that can sting and make a dog dislike tracking.

Finally, some dogs are just not good trackers. Not all dogs are natural trackers, and Schutzhund is not right for all dogs. While most dogs enjoy using their nose, a small percentage just can't handle the problem-solving aspect of tracking and will quit. At this point, you have to ask yourself if you gave the dog enough time to learn during the foundational and motivational stages, or if the dog simply lacks ability.

If you think the problem is the former, go back to the basics with your dog. If it's the latter, no amount of compulsion will turn your dog into a tracker. Accept this, and get another dog for Schutzhund.

Article Indication

Most dogs lie down to indicate an article on the track. Dogs are taught to position themselves with the article between their front legs, but not under their chests. This is the preferred position because it is easier to teach the dog where to position himself in relation to the article and easier to reinforce.

The dog is also allowed to pick up the article and return it to you, and then go on tracking. He is also allowed to sit to indicate the article. Before the tracking begins, you must report to the judge which way the dog will indicate, and the dog must be consistent about it. Points will be deducted if the dog is not.

The problems related to article indication include anticipating or indicating too far in advance, overshooting the article, not indicating at all, false indications and problems indicating articles made of certain materials.

COMMUNICATION ISSUES

In the beginning, you can teach article indication as a separate exercise, away from the actual track. The down is usually taught to indicate an article off the track, to allow for more compulsion—which, it is hoped, won't be transferred to the track. This isn't always the case, which is why you need to be very careful teaching article indication as a separate exercise. It is also important to remember that the dog should respond to the *article, not* the actual command "down."

The other way to teach the articles is on the track. At first, introduce the articles at the *end* of the track. As the dog gets to the end, place a food reward *on* the article and make the dog lie down to eat the food. But even with this method, the dog can sometimes fail to make the association between the article and the command to lie down. In fact, many times dogs and trainers get stuck on a problem with article indication because of poor communication.

To make it easier for the dog, you can teach a specific command for indicating the article, such as "show me" or "find it." This can be especially handy when a dog misses an article. If you tell the dog where the article is and ask him to lie down, the dog didn't work for the article and will not learn that he must find it. A command such as "find it" makes it very clear that you are asking for more than a down.

Another problem may crop up when the dog lies down a few feet short of the article and you give the track command. The dog now thinks he indicated the article correctly and you are asking him to continue tracking. If this isn't confusing enough, many handlers will correct their dog as he sets off down the track, and ask him to down on the missed article. Now the dog has been corrected for the appropriate response to the track command, and asked to down on an article he had no idea he missed!

What we're trying to say is that "track" should mean "put your nose down and follow the track," and "down" should mean lie down, as the dog must do in obedience, and the dog must learn a new command for indicating an article. When you say "find it" or "show me," the dog should do exactly this—not keep tracking forward, and not wait until you find the article and suggest that the dog lie down. "Find it" tells the dog, "find the article yourself!"

Another important part of good communication is making sure your dog fully understands a particular command. You should apply compulsion *only* after you are sure the dog knows what is required. Do not lose your temper and start correcting the dog before he understands what you're expecting. Doing this will lead to the most common problem of all: a dog that doesn't want to track.

FALSE INDICATIONS

Anticipating an article and lying down too quickly is a form of avoidance. The dog may be getting the scent of the article well ahead, and associate the article with compulsion. Therefore, the dog will lie down in order to avoid the correction that he has associated with the article.

If he does this, you need to reassure him that he can go up to the article without a correction or force being applied. You can invite the dog up to the article by walking to him calmly and placing food on it. You can also walk closely behind your dog on the track and encourage him with the command "find it." As the dog gets comfortable with being close to the article, you can ease yourself back to the proper distance.

When dealing with this problem, do not make the dog work article after article on one track. This will only pressure the dog, which was your problem in the first place. Instead, lay a medium-length track with a few articles. The first time the dog indicates correctly, offer plenty of praise and rewards and then end the tracking exercise—which may be the biggest reward of all.

Releasing the dog from tracking at this *high point* makes it really clear what you want. The dog will then understand that indicating correctly makes the pressure go away and brings a reward.

Even though you have set out a few articles, reward and end the exercise if the dog does it right on the first one—don't push your luck by making him find the second one. Once the dog is confident and doing well consistently on the first article, you can go to the next article.

If the dog falsely indicates when the article is not even near, you have a bigger problem. This means he feels really pressured. Go back to the very beginning of tracking training and forget about articles for a while. Have patience—you'll get back to it.

DIFFERENT MATERIALS

To be prepared for competition, your dog must have experience with articles of different sizes made from various materials. The dog should also get used to tracking on the scent of the *material only*. Although in a trial every article should, in theory, have the scent of the track layer, this may not always be so. If the track layer is expected to lay down a lot of tracks on the morning of the trial, he or she may have a big stack of articles. If the articles on your track came out of the middle of the stack, the layer may have handled them very little, and they will not have much scent on them.

Practice using a wide variety of articles that have no scent on them (handle them with gloves), or articles that the track layer has handled only briefly, so your dog will be able to solve this problem on trial day.

OVERSHOOTING

The dog should also learn to look for an article even if it's a foot or so off the track. Sometimes a tracklayer in a hurry will not place an article

Top Terrain Tip

At both national and international trials, it is very common to hear it announced that tracking will be on one type of terrain (alfalfa, for instance), only to find out later that it will be on grass or dirt. If there are more entries, for instance, than there are alfalfa fields, grass may be used. Look around when you arrive, and see if you can find an example of each type of surface to track on before the trial day. If you are not ready for such a change in terrain, even a top tracking dog will not receive full points.

correctly. And it's fairly common to find that an article has blown off the track a bit.

You may also have trouble with something covering the article. A piece of paper or a few leaves may blow over the article. When tracking in high grass, the grass may cover it. If you practice this beforehand, encouraging your dog to solve these problems, you are much better off on the day of the competition.

As with all problem solving, let your dog learn in small steps. Teach your dog to indicate when the article is partially covered in grass. After the dog is successful with this, teach him the same skill with a large article that is fully covered. Be patient. Like everything else, this takes time and experience. The dog must understand the game: that although he will not always *see* the article, something may be there anyway.

When tracking on dirt, make sure you sometimes use articles that are the same color as the dirt. The well-trained dog should not be surprised to find an article in a puddle or at the bottom of a ditch. Practicing on different terrain and with different problems for the dog to solve will make him ready for anything that may happen in a trial.

JUMP STARTING

Jump starting, or rushing to an article, happens when the dog learns to generalize; that is, to anticipate your commands and the actions that will follow. Dogs are masters at reading body language, and a simple movement, such as you getting up or picking up the tracking line, may cue the dog to take off. This generally happens when the dog is feeling anxious.

The solution, then, is to *relieve anxiety* as much as possible. One way is to put your hand on the dog's shoulders or back as you give the command. This steadies the dog and takes his mind off the imperative to rush. While the dog is at the article, you might also take some extra time petting him and giving treats for a job well done. This attention should have the effect of *almost* giving the dog the impression that he is done.

Your intention is to relax the dog to the point where, when you decide to go again, he will not jump off but will continue in a methodical manner. When you set off again, give your command in a quiet, gentle tone. This will reassure the dog that he doesn't have to leap off and rush toward the next article.

Vary your movements so you make yourself less predictable to the dog. Vary the amount of time you will stay at an article and the position you take upon starting to track again; if you normally start off from the right side of your dog, move to the left, or vice versa. Handlers often create a conditioned jump start in a dog with their timing and body language, and shaking up the routine should help the dog understand that things have changed.

Problems on Corners

In 95 percent of cases, a dog that has problems with corners is tracking too fast for his brain to acknowledge the corner. The result usually is that the dog will either circle or proceed straight ahead, thinking that sooner or later you will tell him he missed a corner by correcting him.

Double-laid corners may be used in the beginning to instill confidence, but don't put yourself in a position where you must rely on them. You can also track on easier terrain, where the dog can see the footprints and be successful at turning the corner. Then work on slowing the dog down by using cross-tracks to focus the dog on *your* scent. Initially, use rewards after each cross-track to make sure the dog understands that it is *your scent* that matters, not just *any* footprint he can see on the ground.

A reward may also be placed on an article right after a turn, so there is lots of reinforcement for making the turn correctly. Another possibility is to end the track right after the turn. We discussed this option in the section on false indications, and the reasons for using it are the same.

Ivan Balabanov, Kelly Martin and A'Shane Ot Vitosha, SchHIII, IPOIII, in training before the 1996 North American Championship, where A'Shane got 99 points and High in Tracking.

All these training techniques need to be considered carefully because which one works best will depend on the dog. Whichever method you try, use it a few times to address the problem and then resume normal training. Using these problem-solving techniques too often may lead to other problems, such as false indications after a turn, or speeding after the turn because the dog is looking for the reward.

Your position on corners is important, too. Stay close to your dog when training for the corners to restrict his search radius. This will make it easier for the dog to stay on the right track.

Remember to use different footwork on the turns. Step over at the turn, making a bigger step, to keep the dog aware that if he comes to the end of a track, this must be a corner. And don't insist on neat right angles; the dog should only be concerned with finding the corner, even if he has to circle to find the right direction.

Sometimes the dog has already developed the habit of circling on the corners due to stress or because he is anticipating a correction. It may be helpful to use a prompting technique such as setting up chickenwire fencing shaped like a chute on the corners so the dog cannot circle and does the turn accurately without the stress of being corrected. In most cases, correcting the dog further is unproductive.

When a dog *cuts* a corner, it is generally due to the wind direction. But he may also anticipate a turn when you keep laying the track with pretty much the same length and pattern. In tracking, there should be *no pattern training*, since *real* tracking is anything but that.

Corrections and Rewards

Corrections should be in the form of a short, firm, fast jerk on the training collar. They should be given with just enough force (and no more) to remind your dog to get back to work. This will vary from dog to dog.

The dog's response to a correction *should not be panic.* If it is, either your correction was too severe or the dog didn't understand why he was being corrected. Correction should *never* be given before the dog actually does something wrong—this will discourage the dog from working, and will most likely be a self-fulfilling prophecy.

The perfect setup for fast learning is to *allow the dog to make a mistake and then correct* (preferably only once) with the line. Then let the dog find the track. Don't point it out yourself. Ideally, there will be a reward offered right after the correction when the dog gets back on track. Thus *the dog will be impressed with the outcome of correct behavior.*

To reward instantly, use a second person who walks along and throws bait down onto the track as the situation warrants. This person has to understand which situations warrant such rewards because verbal cues from you will only confuse the dog. If the dog gets too tired or a track becomes unworkable, this person can also end the track. This way, the dog never quits in the middle of a track (something you don't want him to think is a possibility), and yet is never pushed beyond his abilities.

The Schutzhund III Obedience Test

At this level, a dog is required to complete a four-part basic obedience test (heel, sit, down with a recall and stand-stay while heeling) and six advanced exercises. We'll take a look at them one by one, from the point of view of the handler, the dog and the judge.

The rules for all of these exercises are taken from the *United Schutzhund Clubs of America Official Rule Book.* For complete and accurate details, please consult your rule book.

The Basic Obedience Test

HEELING

The Handler

- The handler will report to the judge with the dog heeling off-leash freely. The leash will not be visible to the dog.
- After giving the dog the command to heel, the handler will proceed in a straight line 40 to 50 paces without stopping.
- The handler will perform a left turnabout and, after 10 to 15 paces, do a running exercise and a slow exercise, each for at least 10 paces.

- While heeling at a normal pace, the dog will perform at least one right turn, one left turn and one left turnabout.
- The handler is permitted to use voice commands only when starting the exercise and when changing pace.
- During the halt, the handler is not permitted to change his or her position, and especially shall not step sideways toward the dog.
- Proceeding through the group with the dog in the heel position, the handler is required to stop at least once in the group.

The Dog

- The dog should be willing and outgoing, following the handler upon the heel command.
- The dog should always heel close to the left knee of the handler, with his shoulder blade next to the handler's knee.
- The dog must not forge ahead, move to the side or lag behind.
- A dog that lags, forges, moves sideways or hesitates in the turns is faulty.
- As the handler comes to a stop, the dog should come to a sit position without being influenced by the handler.
- When shots are fired, the dog must remain indifferent to the noise of the gun.
- The dog will be excused immediately if he demonstrates gun insecurity.
- If the dog demonstrates some aggression toward the gunshot, this will be scored as conditionally faulty, as long as the dog remains under the control of the handler. To receive a full score, the dog must be indifferent to the gunshot.

The Judge

- The judge should expect the heel off-leash exercise to be demonstrated to its fullest extent.
- The judge should place a special emphasis on gun indifference.
- Two shots must be fired with a 10-second interval, from a distance of 15 paces.

- The judge will excuse a dog that runs away. If the judge detects gun insecurity, the judge may test the dog with additional gunshots.
- The judge can use the gunshot impartiality test during the heel off-leash and the long down under distraction exercises.

SIT

The Handler

- The handler and his or her free-heeling dog will proceed in a straight line.
- After about 10 paces, the handler will issue the voice command to sit, while not interrupting pace nor facing the dog.
- After another 30 paces, the handler will stop and face the dog.
- When requested by the judge, the handler will return to the dog and assume the basic heeling position on the right side of the dog.

The Dog

- Upon command, the dog should heel free with the handler in a straight line.
- Upon command to sit, the dog should sit promptly and maintain the position as the handler continues to walk away.

The Judge

- Should the dog lie down or remain standing instead of sitting, the judge will deduct up to five points.

DOWN WITH RECALL

The Handler

- From the basic heel position, the handler and free-heeling dog will proceed in a straight line.
- After 10 paces, the handler will begin to run another 10 paces, and will give the "down" command without breaking stride.

- The handler must not influence the dog in any way and, without breaking stride, will move another 40 paces in a straight line before turning around and facing the dog, remaining motionless.
- When approximately 15 seconds have passed and the judge requests, the handler will call the dog to come.

The Dog

- The free-heeling dog should run next to the handler's side and, upon command, must lie down quickly.
- When commanded to come, the dog should come to the handler in a swift and spirited manner, sitting close in front.
- When commanded to heel, the dog should quickly move to a sitting position on the left side of the handler.

The Judge

- Should the dog stand-stay or sit during the exercise, but return on the recall without fault, the judge will deduct up to five points.

STAND-STAY WHILE HEELING

The Handler

- From the basic heel position, the handler, with a free-heeling dog, will proceed forward in a straight line.
- After about 10 paces, the handler will command the dog to stand-stay without breaking stride or looking about.
- After an additional 30 paces, the handler will stop and turn to face the dog.
- When requested by the judge, the handler will return to the dog.

The Dog

- The dog should begin the exercise heeling free in a straight line.
- Upon command from the handler, the dog should stand and stay until the handler returns to him.

The Judge

- Should the dog move from the stand-stay before the handler returns, the judge will deduct points equivalent to the infraction.

Stand-Stay While Running

THE HANDLER

- From the basic heel position, the handler will run with the dog in a straight line.
- The handler will give the "stand-stay" command without breaking stride or looking about.
- After an additional 30 paces, the handler will stop, turn around and face the dog.
- Upon the judge's request, the handler will recall the dog.
- The handler will command the dog to heel, and the dog should move into the sit position at the handler's left side.

THE DOG

- The dog should begin by running in a straight line in the heel position next to the handler.
- When commanded to do so, the dog should stop and stand.
- When the handler recalls the dog, the dog should come to the handler with a spirited and swift motion, and sit in front.
- Upon the command to heel, the dog should move quickly to the sit position on the handler's left side.

THE JUDGE

- The judge will deduct up to five points if the dog sits or lies down after the stand command is given.
- The judge will consider as faulty any of the following:

  1. The dog moving toward the handler
  2. The handler looking around
  3. The dog slowing on the recall

- The judge may score with half points.

Retrieving a Dumbbell on Level Ground

THE HANDLER

- The handler will start the exercise with the dog sitting in the heel position.
- The handler will toss the dumbbell about 10 paces away.
- The handler will give the voice command for the dog to retrieve the dumbbell.
- The handler will pause after the dog brings back the dumbbell, then issue the command to release and take the dumbbell from the dog.
- The handler must remain in the basic position as the command to heel is given and while the dog returns to the heel position.

THE DOG

- The dog, sitting freely next to the handler, should, on command, quickly move to the dumbbell that has been thrown.
- The dog must immediately and quickly pick up and retrieve the dumbbell, taking it to the handler.
- The dog must bring the dumbbell and sit closely in front of the handler.
- The dog must release the dumbbell to the handler on command.
- The dog must, on command, move to the heel position at the handler's left side and sit.

THE JUDGE

- The dumbbell shall weigh two kilograms.
- The judge may deduct up to four points from a dog that drops, mouths or plays with the dumbbell.
- A judge may deduct up to three points for a handler who changes the basic position.
- The judge will score the exercise with a zero if the dog does not retrieve the dumbbell.

Retrieving a Dumbbell Over a Brush Hurdle

THE HANDLER

- The handler will take a position an acceptable distance in front of the hurdle, with the dog sitting freely in the heel position.
- The handler will throw the dumbbell to the other side of the jump. The handler may repeat the throw with the judge's permission, if necessary.
- Before the dog reaches the dumbbell, the handler will command the dog to retrieve it.
- After the dog has returned with the dumbbell, the handler will pause briefly and then take the dumbbell from the dog with a command to let go.
- The handler must remain in the basic position until the dog comes to the heel position.

THE DOG

- The dog should start the exercise sitting freely in the heel position next to the handler.
- Upon a voice command, the dog must clear the hurdle without touching it, pick up the dumbbell, return to the handler over the jump and sit closely, facing the handler.
- The dog must remain holding the dumbbell in his mouth until commanded to let go.
- Upon command to heel, the dog should move into the heel position and immediately sit.

THE JUDGE

- The dumbbell shall weigh 650 grams, and the brush hurdle shall be 1 meter high and 1.5 meters wide.
- The judge may deduct up to two points for slightly brushing the hurdle, and up to three points for strongly brushing or stepping on the hurdle.

Schutzhund is a sport for everyone! Will Adams doesn't let his physical challenges keep him from throwing the dumbbell over the hurdle.

- The judge may penalize the dog up to four points for dropping, playing with or mouthing the dumbbell.
- This exercise has many possible faults and deductions. For the best information, see the official rule book.

Climb-Jump Over the Inclined Wall and Retrieve an Object

THE HANDLER

- The handler will begin from a position an acceptable distance in front of the inclined wall, with the dog sitting in the heel position.
- The handler will throw the dumbbell to the other side of the jump. The handler may repeat the throw with the judge's permission, if necessary.
- The handler will give the dog a voice command to retrieve the dumbbell. The command must be given before the dog picks up the dumbbell.
- After the dog has returned with the dumbbell, the handler will pause briefly and then remove the dumbbell from the dog's mouth with a command to let go.

THE DOG

- The dog should begin the exercise sitting freely in the heel position.
- Upon voice command, the dog must clear the hurdle without touching it, pick up the dumbbell and return to the handler over the jump.
- The dog should arrive with the dumbbell in his mouth, and sit closely in front of the handler.
- Upon command, the dog must release the dumbbell to the handler.
- Upon command, the dog should come quickly into the heel position.

THE JUDGE

- The inclined wall shall be 1.8 meters high and 1.3 meters wide at the bottom.
- In the case of a clumsy toss by the handler, or due to strong wind conditions, the dumbbell may land off to the side. At the handler's discretion, he or she may ask the judge's permission to retrieve the dumbbell and rethrow it. There will be no point deductions for this.
- Should the dog drop the dumbbell, it should be determined whether the dog dropped it due to nonchalance, laziness or strong temperamental drive. Should there be any doubt, the judge may ask for a repeat of the exercise.
- This exercise has many possible faults and deductions. For the best information see the official rule book.

Go Ahead and Down

THE HANDLER

- From the basic heel position, the handler, with a free-heeling dog, will proceed forward in the designated direction for several paces.
- The handler will command the dog to go out. This should be executed by lifting the arm while stopping.
- After the dog goes out about 40 paces, the handler will command the dog to lie down. The handler may hold up an arm in the designated direction until the dog has lain down.
- Upon the judge's request, the handler will proceed forward to the right side of the dog and command the dog to sit.

THE DOG

- The dog should heel freely next to the handler in the designated direction. At the command to go out, the dog should proceed in a straight line, at a fast pace, for at least 40 paces.
- The dog must lie down quickly at the down command.
- After the handler moves into the heel position, the dog should rise to a sitting position on command.

THE JUDGE

- Repeatedly lifting the arm to signal the dog is not permitted.
- The dog must move in a straight line; however, a slight deviation is not faulty.
- Strong deviations to the side, too short a distance, reluctance to lie down, anticipating the down command, or getting up early will result in point deductions.

Long Down With Distractions

THE HANDLER

- In this exercise, the dog must lie down while another dog performs obedience exercises nearby. Before the other dog begins, the handler will command the dog to lie down in a spot designated by the judge.
- Without turning, the handler will proceed about 40 paces, out of sight of the dog yet still on the training field.
- When requested by the judge, the handler will return to the dog by moving to the right side of the dog and commanding the dog to sit.

THE DOG

- The dog should lie down in the spot designated by the handler and remain there as the handler moves out of sight.
- The dog should remain down and stay in the designated spot while the dog on the field completes the obedience exercises.
- The dog should rise into a sitting position when commanded by the returning handler.

THE JUDGE

- The handler must remain out of sight until the judge requests him or her to return to the dog.
- The judge should fault restless behavior on the part of the handler, hidden help or the dog getting up prematurely.

- The judge will give a partial score if the dog stands or sits up but remains in the spot.
- If the dog moves more than three meters before the other dog on the field has completed five exercises, the score will be zero.
- If the dog moves more than three meters after the other dog on the field has completed five exercises, a partial score is in order.
- If the dog moves to meet the returning handler, three points should be deducted.

What the Judge Wants to See

The judge is looking for speed, focus and precision, but that's not all. The factor that will have perhaps the biggest impact on your routine is the way you and your dog interact. The obedience exercises should look like a well-choreographed dance. You must also be able to follow the judge's requests and maintain the dog's motivation using only verbal praise.

Everything from the way you play with your dog to how you train your dog can be reflected in the dog's performance at trials. It is our belief that through *motivational training* the dog will be able to show his full potential and spirit.

Using strong compulsion-based methods can also get the job done. The sport has become so highly competitive, however, that a judge with a good eye can tell whether a dog is working through avoidance or motivation. Both dogs might perform at the same speed and level of correctness, but the one working through avoidance will tend to cower, lay his ears back and in other ways show avoidance behavior. A good judge favors an eager, self-assured dog working out of joy and willingness. A dog that appears to be under pressure from the handler will not score as well in the end. This is important because the obedience score can make or break a competitor.

Using Deprivation in Obedience Training

We are assuming at this level of Schutzhund training that you already know how to teach the basic obedience exercises required for Schutzhund I through III. Here we are talking about a philosophy and training method that can put you at the top of competition.

Deprivation of food, exercise, unconditional attention and play are all useful tools in conditioning a top performance. This means deprivation in *small doses*, and never to an extent that will harm the dog.

FOOD DEPRIVATION

If you just finished tracking and have used two packs of hotdogs as rewards on the track, your dog will be full and less stimulated by food. To use food rewards to motivate the dog in obedience immediately afterward would be less than ideal. Even if the dog takes the food, the reward will be less valuable because his needs have already been met.

The rule of thumb is not to feed the dog for at least six hours before training. In some cases, skipping the evening meal the night before an early morning training session is the best course of action.

PLAY AND EXERCISE DEPRIVATION

As with food deprivation, a dog that has just played Frisbee for half an hour is not going to be as motivated to do a quick and straight recall for a toy reward. Again, the need has already been satisfied and the desire will be less.

The idea is to make the dog relax and restrict his free movement. Some trainers will kennel or crate their dog several hours before training. When the dog comes out, the pent-up energy can be funneled into training. It is also possible to keep the dog with you, inside the house or hotel, and restrict him to a minimum of activity.

A good rule of thumb is that a dog should not be confined to a crate more than a total of 8 hours in a 24-hour period. This may be helpful when preparing for a trial. Use your judgment when deciding how long to confine the dog, taking into account his age and energy level. On average, crating the dog for two hours before training will be enough.

SOCIAL DEPRIVATION

Giving the dog unconditional attention in the form of petting and social interaction with other dogs or humans, or allowing him free run of the house, including following you from room to room, can also lessen the dog's intensity when he works. If the dog has already gained attention from you by just existing, why should he work to please you?

This is why it's a good idea to use a crate to keep the dog comfortably in the house without being your constant companion. Again, this is an aid to training. It is not meant to be overused.

Using Food and Play Training

We teach new obedience exercises using food rewards. This keeps the dog calm, and the reward helps the dog focus. At first, every correct response is rewarded. But as the dog shows a consistent response, the food reward becomes intermittent.

Intermittent rewards, whether food or toys, condition a dog to work longer and harder. The dog should be able to do a whole sequence of behaviors with praise as the only reinforcement. This will happen when the dog doesn't know when he will get his primary reward.

Eventually the food reward will be replaced by toy rewards. But before going to this step, you must be sure the dog knows the command. Dogs are masters at reading body language, and your dog may be reading some subtle physical sign that you are not even aware of, rather than responding to your verbal command. To test this, face away from your dog and look up at the sky while giving the command. If your dog still performs the command, you can go on to the next step.

To achieve faster responses from the dog every time, we will now go to toy rewards. It is through play that you can gain the fastest response when a command is given. The dog will perform without avoidance behavior and will visibly exude eagerness to work.

We strongly believe in teaching the dog to play with anything handy. This way, if you forget to bring a certain toy, you can improvise with your hat, a plastic milk jug, a stick (be careful of injury) or any available object. What you are playing with is not the reward; rather, it is the satisfaction of the interaction between dog and trainer.

In using play effectively, it is important that the dog learn to play *with you* when the reward is given. If the dog runs away and plays with the toy on his own, you will lose the timing necessary to keep the focus on the exercise. The dog needs to know that the fun comes from *you*. It is *you* who makes the toy move, and *you* who plays tug. This way, the dog learns to stay focused on you when the toy is given.

We are now ready to teach the "out" command. The dog needs to learn that you play a *short* game of tug with the toy and then you expect

In order to work, the dog must have the desire to play. (Nanette Nickherson)

a release on command. Any obedience command should be given before the toy goes in motion. This teaches the dog that a quick sit, down or other command makes the game begin—in other words, *his obedience* controls the use of the toy. It creates a willingness in the dog and a confidence, as well.

To teach "out," first tease the dog with the toy; let him bite it and play tug. To get the dog to release, stop moving or playing with the toy, offer food and give the command "out" at the same time. Stopping all movement of the toy will be helpful later when teaching the dog not to bite a stationary object.

It is important to keep the toy in the dog's sight but not moving while he is eating his food reward. To further reward the out, the toy then comes to life and the dog again gets to play.

Teaching the dog to come to you when he gets a toy reward is a crucial skill for obedience work. For this we like to use only one toy, rather than the common method of throwing one toy and replacing it with another. It is important that the dog knows you control the game and you don't have to cheat to do it. The dog should play with you, bringing the toy directly to you and outing it on command. The dog should learn to think, "I see the toy; how can I please him so that I will get to play?" instead of, "I see the toy; what if I just grab it from his hand and take off with it?"

At this point you are ready to move on to the actual obedience exercises. You can now start to apply corrections when the dog is overly distracted from the exercise. A good handler should know the necessary amount of correction for their particular dog, and should always offer the least severe correction possible.

A good handler should also be able to judge from zero to 100 what percentage of the dog's drive is being used. The reward can be manipulated to turn up the drive. How and when a handler rewards their dog will vary based on that particular dog and what is necessary to bring about the best performance. This can vary from dog to dog and from day to day, and is more of an art than a science.

Problem Solving in Advanced Obedience

The obedience test is a series of complex maneuvers that, when performed well, look like a carefully choreographed dance between dog and handler. With so many individual exercises, there is a lot that can go wrong. But problems do fall into some broad categories, which we'll look at here.

Position and Eye Contact

As we mentioned in Chapter 6 on tracking problems, sometimes mistakes are caused by poor communication between handler and dog. Using "watch" or a similar command to teach eye contact between you and your dog is important—not just because it makes a nice picture to look at, but because it will focus the dog's attention on you, which will facilitate communication in all exercises.

The most popular way to teach this command is to hold a bit of food or a toy up near your left shoulder so that the dog looks up at it. The problem is that most dogs will look at the toy or the food but will not make eye contact with you. What you end up with is a false watch, where the head is up but there is no eye contact.

What's happening here is that the dog is watching the reward. This brings him slightly in front of you, where he tends to crowd you as he tries to get to the reward. Now the dog will be crooked on finishes, sits and even downs and stands. He will also tend to forge in front of you.

This positioning problem can become so difficult that some handlers will resort to devices such as knee spikes—objects strapped to the handler's knees with spikes sticking out that prevent the dog from crowding. This creates a really unfortunate dilemma for the dog. On the one hand, the toy or food at the shoulder is reinforcing the crowding, but at the same time you are constantly correcting the dog for pushing into you. So the same behavior is both reinforced and corrected. Such conflicting messages make it very difficult for the dog to perform correctly. Most dogs will actually view the correction not as a correction, but as something that happens routinely when heeling.

If you use a different technique to train the watch, you can avoid these problems altogether. This is one of the differences between Ivan's approach and that of most other trainers. This approach makes it much clearer to the dog what is being asked of him. The idea is to teach eye contact, plain and simple. This isn't a difficult concept for dogs to understand. In fact, they get the idea very quickly.

Eye contact means meeting the eyes of the handler. The dog can be in *any* position for this. The position is not important, since you only need the dog to understand that if he looks *directly into your eyes,* he gets the treat.

Within a few training sessions, you should be able to hold a treat near the dog or in any position because the dog understands that the focus is on your eyes, not the treat. The dog should understand that the quickest way to get the treat is not to grab it from you, but rather to look in your eyes. You will use the word "watch" for this. If you have used "watch" previously and the dog has been looking at the food or toy, we recommend changing the command word to something else, so you do not confuse him. As with the other commands, food rewards are used at first to teach the command. Once the dog understands, switch to a tug, a toy or a ball.

The "watch" exercise always begins from a stationary position. By doing this, you can focus on just one concern at a time. If you are in motion, you also have to be concerned with leaning, forging and so on. It is important to go slowly and focus on one issue at a time.

Martha Hoffman's Amok Ot Vitosha, SchHIII, IPOIII, at the 1997 North American Championships, where he took High in Obedience with 98 points. Note how intensely he watches Martha. (Nanette Nickherson)

Begin by keeping the toy or food in your hand right in front of the dog. He will most likely be very focused on your hand, for obvious reasons. Give him some time to try to get to the food. Once he sees that you are not giving it to him, he may actually look at you wondering what's going on. This is the time to praise him and give him the treat. If it seems the dog doesn't want to look at you, you may use his name or some other noise to get his attention for just a second so you can reward the eye contact.

Another way of doing this is to have the dog sit beside you and physically tilt his head up so that he makes eye contact and you can reward him. Then you can start using the command "watch" and ask for longer eye contact.

A common mistake when training this way is to hide the reward from the dog, perhaps behind your back or by your side. This will actually create more interest for the reward, which is not what you want.

After the dog maintains eye contact when the food is visible and within his reach, it's time to start moving the reward around his head, then hiding it, then showing it again and asking for the same response. At this stage, if you are using a toy, tap it gently against the dog's chest and correct the dog lightly if he looks at the toy. Reward him for looking at *you*. It is through repetition, not correction alone, that the dog learns the rules of the game.

Once you're *absolutely sure* the dog knows the rules, you can begin using movement. The reward is now a little harder to get. For instance, watching will not be enough to get the reward if the dog's position isn't correct as well. In this way, you begin to gradually ask more from him.

ADDING DISTRACTIONS

The obedience part of Schutzhund is all about motivation, reliability and correctness. Your worst enemies are distractions.

It is those times when the dog is distracted that some handlers give severe physical corrections that result in ongoing avoidance behaviors from their dogs. It can take months to bring a dog back from a severe correction, if ever. Even then, the dog may still react to distractions, which teaches us that we gain little, if anything, by giving a severe correction.

A'Shane Ot Vitosha, SchH, IPO III, guarding the helper at the 1997 DVG Nationals. (Martha Hoffman)

Nakita Des Deux Pottois, SchHIII, IPOIII, FH, a Malinois, taking High Score in Protection at the USA Nationals 1995. (Doug Loving)

A'Shane Ot Vitosha, SchHIII, IPOIII, at the 1996 Nationals, where he was first American Bred and Trained Dog, and High in Obedience. (Doug Loving)

A brave dog is a thrill to watch in the Schutzhund III advanced protection test. (Doug Loving)

Encouraging the dog to work with his prey drive by using a line attached to the sleeve. The sleeve then simulates the movement of natural prey. (Debbie Dilley)

Bocca Ot Vitosha, SchHIII, and David Delessagas are working in full fighting drive.
(Nanette Nickherson)

*Ivan Balabanov and Bocca Ot Vitosha, SchHIII, on the re-attack after the courage test.
(Nanette Nickherson)*

Kelly Martin's A'Shane Ot Vitosha, SchHIII, IPOIII, taking High in Tracking with 100 points at the 1997 DVG Nationals. (Nanette Nickherson)

Ivan Balabanov and Django Ot Vitosha at seven months. The dog watches Ivan, not the toy. (Nanette Nickherson)

Once the dog can perform the "watch" command in a static position, we start asking for the same attention while heeling. (Nanette Nickherson)

At the opposite end of the spectrum, operant conditioning using negative punishment and positive reinforcement will make the dog perform *better* with distractions. Let's talk about how it works.

By now, you have been practicing the "watch" command at home and the dog should know the rules for playing with you. Your goal is to teach the dog that the training field is a *fun* place, but it is also a place to focus on *you*. It is easy for your dog to lose interest in you and focus on new scents, people, other dogs, anything.

This is why we try to condition dogs as puppies to pay attention only to us any place we decide to work with them. This happens gradually. First we make sure the dog has the desire to play with whatever we're offering. Then we take him to various places—first in the house, then the backyard, then the training field when no one else is on it. We try to keep his interest on us by playing for a few minutes and then quickly taking him away from that environment.

A few minutes after the short play session, we may take the dog out once again to the place where we played, but this time without asking him to do anything. This gives him a chance to explore and see where he was. He may want to initiate a play session, but at this time it is important not to get involved. Then he won't want to waste any of the time that we do play with him.

To help him even more, as we take him out of the crate we start adding a cue command such as "let's play." The key thing we are trying to achieve is the ability to bring the dog into any type of environment and let him know that it's playtime.

Next, we gradually start adding distractions, and show the dog through negative punishment that he can only play with his handler. You will need the cooperation of other handlers and dogs that you know and trust. You must talk to them about what you plan to do. Your goal is to teach your dog to focus only on you, even in the presence of other dogs that are working for *their* rewards. At first, there will be a natural conflict in your dog. He'll want to go see the other dog and handler, and be involved in *their* game. Rather than fight this tendency by correcting your dog, you can permanently resolve this conflict by allowing your dog to do what he wants. This may seem counterintuitive, but let's look at an example of how it works.

The other dog and handler should be a seasoned team that you can trust. They are playing a game of toss and fetch, and your dog becomes excited. You allow your dog to run over and attempt to get into the game. As your dog approaches, the handler picks up the toy and walks away from your dog. The handler's dog comes along, and both ignore your dog. At the same time, you begin to toss your dog's toy into the air and call his name. When he returns to you and his toy, you play with him.

Do this several times and your dog will soon learn that *you* are the center of the universe, not other dogs and handlers. The dog also learns that his own handler and toy are his, and other dogs have theirs. Other dogs' handlers and toys are not rewarding. This is a *natural learning experience* for the dog, and erases all conflict in your dog's mind about this type of distraction. You will never have to fight with your dog about it again.

This exercise also benefits the well-trained dog that is assisting you. That dog's handler is teaching him that although other dogs might want to share his toy, it is best not to let them. This makes the dog work harder for the toy because it's something other dogs would like to have. The other dog will work harder to keep his handler's attention, too, because the play has become a competition.

This whole training process keeps the right mood on the training field because the dogs do not feel they are being isolated from one another. They can go toward each other, but they choose not to because they have learned there is nothing fun for them there.

This does not mean compulsion is never used to correct distractions. It is used when necessary. However, the conditioning process makes it necessary much less often.

The Heel

It's easy to forget how difficult heeling can be. The dog must follow your every move, being supremely sensitive to your body language, while at the same time remaining in a precise position relative to you.

CROWDING

The most common problems during the heel exercise are pushing and crowding. When a dog pushes into you as he walks, it's difficult for you to walk. It also takes away precision on the turns. This is especially true on the left turns.

Dogs can learn to crowd by the way the reward is presented. If you try to keep the dog excited by constantly moving the reward and making wide right circles, the dog may push into you to get to the reward. Another way you can create this problem is by correcting the dog for being distracted by physically pulling him toward you, then rewarding the dog once he is paying attention. The dog may think moving in toward you received the reward.

Ideally, the dog should walk parallel to you. This is accomplished by teaching him to make correct left turns without cutting in front of you. As you make the left turn, the dog should pivot his rear to line up correctly with you *before* he takes a step forward.

To teach this properly, the dog must already know the "watch" command. Before you start to heel while walking, you must teach the dog to correctly move his rear end when making turns in a more static exercise. The goal is not to allow the dog to come straight into you.

Put the dog on a sit. Position yourself as though you have already made the 90-degree turn, so that you and the dog are facing different directions. You should be within an arm's reach of the dog's head. Reach down to the end of the leash with your left hand. The thumb should be underneath the leash, and the fingers on top. Give the heel command and then slowly pull the dog backward as you also step back with your left leg. The left hand that is guiding the dog should move back alongside the moving leg.

Once the step back is completed, use your hand on the leash to twist the collar counterclockwise. This will force the dog to swing his rear end in order to move and line up with your left leg. After the dog is lined up, keep the leash taut and step forward with your left leg into the finish position.

This exercise should be repeated several times in slow motion, until the dog starts to understand what is being asked of him. You can now begin closing the starting distance between you and your dog. Soon you will be starting this exercise still facing different directions, but next to each other.

The finish, when the dog lines up with you, will affect the way he heels. If the dog finishes slightly in front of you, he will be forging when he heels, too. Make sure he is in line with you before adding the heel exercise after the left turn. If the dog does forge at any time, correct the problem by making left turns and insisting that the dog line up correctly before starting off again.

We encourage you to pay attention to your body language on the turns. Be consistent, so you don't keep the dog guessing about what you will do next. For instance, if your head always turns before you make a left or right turn, this can be a cue for the dog. A look to the left cues the dog that you are about to turn left. A look to the right indicates a right turn, and so on. To see if your dog has learned your body language, try walking straight ahead and suddenly look left. Your dog should automatically move his rear end left, as in a turn.

The worst thing you can do is just walk up and down the field without any clear body language. This makes the dog guess if you are going to make a left, a right or an about turn. Even though the dog will learn

LiLiana Varbanov and Boril Ot Vitosha, SchHII, demonstrate teaching the dog to move his rear. Start at a right angle to your dog, and reach down the leash.

Take a step back with your left leg, using the left hand to guide the dog back with you at the same time. Make sure you do not allow the dog to go forward; the first steps he makes should be backwards following your leg.

Twist the collar counterclockwise so that the dog must swing his rear end to line up with your left leg. (Nanette Nickherson)

to heel with you, he will always have an unclear picture of what is required. The end result will be a loss of points in competition.

Practicing endurance in the focused heeling exercise is also important, since you will need attentive, correct work. We suggest combining working on the heel exercises with a lot of retrieving games, going back and forth between heeling and playing. When the dog gets tired, try practicing the static "watch" from the heel position (with the dog sitting next to you) so the dog can rest a bit while still working.

THE RIGHT SPEED

The speed at which you walk on the field has to be comfortable for both the dog and you. Generally speaking, the faster you walk, the better the picture you present. You should not, however, look as if you and the dog are in a race. Walking at a brisk pace helps to keep the dog in drive. The intensity and drive that *you* exude is passed on to the dog. If you also work in drive, you will promote a better attitude in the dog.

As we just mentioned, body language is extremely important on the field. This does not mean cheating. Rather, it is the subtle signals that only a dog that practices day after day with the same handler can pick up on. When done properly, it looks like a dance. Work on developing your cues for speeding up or slowing down the heel. Use them consistently in practice so that your dog can learn exactly what you want. When your dog learns to pick up on your subtle cues, changing pace is easy.

Reaction to the Gunshot

The gun test is used to evaluate a dog's temperament. A fearful reaction to a sudden loud noise is an undesirable trait because it indicates an unstable nervous system. When a dog reacts fearfully to the gunshot, he will almost always show many other weaknesses in his work.

A fearful reaction is considered a genetic trait, so even though there are a few suggestions on how to minimize this by conditioning, they are rarely successful in the long term. The only time we would want to work with this problem is when the gun excites the dog and brings him into drive. Then we use a food reward following the gunshot, which tends to calm the dog. A toy reward as a distraction may also work.

The excitability problem can be solved in a few sessions. The first step is to show your dog where the noise is coming from. Many times the sight of the gun by itself is what triggers the excited-aggressive response, and getting your dog used to it may be all that's needed. You can tie your dog on a long line and get two guns, one loaded and one not. Play tug with the dog without putting any tension on the line (the line is just for security and safety—you don't want to chase your dog as you try to desensitize him). After some play, sit with your dog. We would not use the down because most likely the dog has associated the down with the gun and aggression. Show the unloaded gun to the dog, and let him sniff it if he wants to. Then put the gun away and reward the dog with food, then a game of tug.

Next time, sit with the dog again, show him the gun and let him sniff it, and reward him with food. After clearing the gun (that is, making sure it is not loaded), dry fire it. (Dry firing means simulating firing the gun by cocking the hammer back and pulling the trigger.) This will create a mechanical click. Do this right in front of the dog and give him food. Then put the gun away and play.

It's important every time the dog sees the gun or hears the gun to reward him with food and not the toy. The toy can come *after* the food to release stress, if the dog shows any, and to distract him from the gun.

Next, dry fire the gun a few times and let him sniff. It's important not to stay at this stage for too long, or the dog may be even more surprised to hear the gunshot later. If you don't see any nervousness, go ahead to the next step. Show the dog a loaded gun, and then reward him with food. Sit the dog, move about 10 feet away and show the dog the gun by your side. Go back and give him food, then step away and, if you see that the dog is calm, fire. Go back and give him food, and let him sniff the gun. This time the gun will have the scent of being fired. Give the dog food again, then put the gun away and play tug.

Start building from there. You want to be able to fire a few times and watch your dog's response. He should be looking for food and not seem concerned about the gun. When you've reached that point, have a second person take the gun, let the dog sniff it, have the person fire it and give the gun back to you. Continue the routine of giving a food reward, putting the gun away and playing tug until the dog is comfortable. Progress gradually to a simulation of the actual gun test, where the dog can heel or stay on a down while the gun is being fired. As part of this gradual process, start with a small caliber weapon and gradually move up to a larger caliber as the dog becomes more gun sure.

The Group

Going through the group can be very different from trial to trial. The people in the group may be almost static, or they may be vigorously walking and passing each other. They can circle or move in any number of directions. You are allowed to choose which way to enter the group and where to stop, as long as you and the dog make a figure eight. There are several factors at work here: how you trained your dog, how focused he is, how precise, whether he tends to forge or lag, and so on.

We do not work this exercise before we have taught the turns described earlier in this chapter, where the dog moves his rear in sync with the handler and stays tightly focused. This will be important for the figure eight.

We train the dog to enter from the outside as well as the inside—taking a left or right turn into the group. Usually this decision is made at the very last minute by observing your dog's heeling on the field. If you

Glenn Stevenson and Fax go through the group at the 1994 FCI Championship in Italy.

are paying attention to your dog and see that he's forging ahead, making a left turn is probably the better choice.

It is important not to praise the dog inside the group during a trial because the exercise is not over yet. The group is just one part of the heeling exercise, and you need to complete the entire exercise before you praise your dog.

Don't practice the group exercise with the same people all the time. You don't want the dog to generalize any of the situations or people. For this reason, it is important to practice for "the late group." Sometimes in trials there is a miscommunication and the group isn't ready. Usually in these cases the group will rush to get into position. This rushing may confuse the dog, and the result may be a loss of points. If you've practiced in a variety of settings and scenarios, your dog will be ready for whatever happens.

The Positions

If you reward the sit, down and stand after every quickly accomplished position change, the dog will learn to hit the right position with spirit and energy. This will make it much easier to go to the next step, which is changing position in motion.

Before you teach the change of position in motion, you should first proof your dog to make sure he understands the commands, and is not just responding to subtle changes in your body language. You do this by turning your back on your dog and then giving the command. If the dog responds correctly, he knows the command and is not responding to some other subtle clue you are giving.

Start conditioning the dog to obey commands while you're in motion—do not walk away before giving the command nor stand still as the command is given. Give the command as you walk, just the way it should be done in competition.

Start from the heel position. When you issue the command and the dog hits the desired position, come back and reward him immediately with a game of tug or with food. When this is no longer difficult for the dog, you will ask a little more. Give the command and walk a few more steps. Then, as long as the dog stays, you can reward him. Next time, go out farther from him, and so on.

SIT AND DOWN COMMANDS

The sit is probably the first command your dog learned, and is also the command used most in his everyday life. Curiously enough, it is also the position the greatest percentage of dogs miss at trials. Although this section will use the problem sit as an example, the methods are similar for working on the down.

Before we get to problem solving, let's go over what you should look for in a dog's sit or down. In a sit you want the dog to move his front feet back, rather than moving his rear end forward to complete the position. When this is done out of motion, the dog will not take extra steps forward and will almost jump back into the sit. This will improve the speed of execution.

When you teach the down, ask the dog not to crawl forward, but to keep his front feet in the same spot and move his body back in order to lie down.

To teach the dog to sit or down this way, turn the training into a game that the dog actually likes. The same method can be used as a warm-up to other training or before competition to get the dog into drive. Start by teasing the dog with a toy, moving it around to get his attention. Just before giving the sit command, move directly in front of him and cease movement, not letting him go forward. Then lure him into position with the toy or food. When done properly and with several repetitions, your dog should be moving backward as he obeys the series of commands.

A common reason why dogs do not sit at trials is that they have been corrected a great deal on other positions or when the stand is introduced later in training. For example, suppose the dog isn't performing well in the running stand. Most likely he is trying other behaviors, such as sitting or lying down. If strong corrections are used, in his mind he is being corrected for that sit or down. This will confuse him later when you ask him to perform the command.

When a dog has a problem with one position, it is still important to continue working on those he knows well. This prevents him from presuming that one particular command is safe and that all other commands are associated with corrections. It also gives him a chance to be successful and rewarded. Session after session of running stands will only put more pressure on a dog that performs them poorly. You must concentrate on how to help the dog be successful, rather than on correcting him every time he makes a mistake.

Begin by building drive.

The dog obeys the command in an instant.

A quick reward to reinforce the command.
(Nanette Nickherson)

Prolonged reward will also help with problem commands. For example, if you are satisfied with your dog's sit, release him and play a fetch game for few minutes. Keep the dog in the same mood and ask for the command one more time. Give a lot of play and then end your session. The dog then sees the command he's having a problem with as a direct cue to the biggest reward you can give—turning the session into playtime.

To make this concept even more clear, start the session with the dog really feeling relaxed, comfortable and successful. If the dog is doing fine as the session progresses, ask for the problem command. The dog may initially be very hesitant. You can help a lot—even gently place the dog into position. End the session with play that is clearly a result of this particular command. You can also ask for the command before feeding the dog.

A consistent voice inflection is necessary when you give commands. Most trainers use a very low voice when giving the down command, moderate for the sit and a high-pitched or almost silent command for the stand. This makes the dog cue on the tone of voice as well as the command itself, making him more self-assured when obeying it. You shouldn't try to mimic someone else, though. Each person has their own way of speaking. Try to teach your dog to respond to the commands in the tone of voice that feels right for you.

Another thing to consider is that your dog may miss a position only because he hasn't had much exposure to a particular environment. Some judges watch you from a short distance, motionless. Others will walk right by your side or come very close to the dog as you give the command, and use a lot of hand gestures or a loud voice when guiding you through the sequence. This will create a certain level of distraction for your dog. That's why it's so very important to have different people and various distractions on the field when you practice obedience. Of course, the dog will perform better when you're alone or with a friend that the dog is accustomed to. Some trainers avoid strong distractions during training, but this is a mistake. You'll have to face all kinds of situations while competing, and you and the dog might as well get used to them.

Commands in Motion

Unlike with heeling, giving body cues here can be your worst enemy. In training everything may look great, but on the day of the trial if you feel stiff or can't bend your shoulder or nod your head as you normally would, your dog won't sit or down. That's why as soon as your dog understands a command, you need to stop the physical clues.

This is one of the hardest things for trainers to change. Just like dogs, trainers also become conditioned, especially when something is working. The best way to find out how you both look on the field is to have a training session videotaped. This gives you the opportunity to see from the sidelines, which is different than someone telling you what's going on while you are doing it. You see how the dog responds, how much help you give, your timing and all the other aspects of your performance.

In training, try not to let the dog anticipate what's next. Avoid establishing a pattern in your routines and use a variable reward schedule. When the dog is first learning a command, reward him as soon as he completes it, but once he has learned a skill it is important to keep the dog guessing about when the reward will come. This will keep his interest and motivation high. In laboratory studies it has been proven that animals on irregular schedules, for both the rewards and the work, will work harder and harder without losing attention or desire to do the job.

If you are still having trouble with commands in motion, it may help to use a long line and a second person. If the dog is confused about the exercise, correcting him is useless—he doesn't know what you want. It's therefore essential to help him succeed, and another person can do that. The person holding the second line does *not* correct, but prevents the dog from continuing forward. After several tries with rewards, even though you're helping a lot, the dog will relax and become more reliable. Playing with a toy is still our favorite reward because the dog is put in drive and is willing to work in order to get the toy.

Remember to practice *all* the positions, rather than repeating one or two commands for a whole session. The best advice is to go slowly and allow your training to play out over several sessions, rather than trying to make one training session perfect.

THE SIT IN MOTION

To avoid or correct a slow sit in motion, it's important to be clear about what you are rewarding and what you are punishing. For example, if you perform the sit in motion as it will be done in a trial and you reward at the end of the routine, you are actually rewarding only the "stay" portion of the exercise, even if the dog had a quick sit response. The fast sit behavior is not reinforced and the dog will not learn that speed is important.

You can gauge how your training is going by observing the dog's reactions when you're going back to him after the sit in motion. If the dog is looking away as you approach, or yawns, he is slightly nervous and doesn't want to make a mistake. This is not necessarily a bad thing. When the dog lifts one of his feet at the same time that he's looking away, it's a sign that he's under too much stress and you need to loosen up with this exercise.

A dog experiencing too much stress cannot perform well. How can you relieve the stress without letting the dog develop sloppy obedience work? Try a simple change in routine, such as going around the dog from the side opposite the one you normally use. Avoiding eye contact as you go back is another idea. Once we know this is a problem, our favorite solution is to throw the dog a toy just before he usually displays stress. Be careful not to overuse this once your dog is relaxed, or he will soon realize that by looking away he can make you initiate a game.

THE DOWN IN MOTION

As with the sit in motion, and indeed all commands, you must be aware of what you are rewarding or correcting during the down in motion. On the down, be careful not to reward the dog before he completes the position. You want his elbows to touch the ground before you reward him, or else you will have sloppy downs to work on.

Remember, that to the dog, the recall is a reward in this exercise. If the dog has a very strong desire to be recalled, it is not necessary for him to perform the recall every time he is down. You can consider the down and the recall to be two separate training exercises.

THE STAND IN MOTION

Most people are accustomed to seeing a belly strap used to teach a dog to stand. The strap is wrapped under the dog's belly so that he cannot sit. When the dog no longer resists, you don't need to use it anymore. This works well with some dogs, but others become so preoccupied with the strap that it inhibits learning the command.

Regardless of whether you use a belly strap, start teaching the stand in slow motion. With the dog at the heel, gradually slow down. Slowing *gradually* is important because you do not want the dog to think you are stopping and automatically sit. You can try holding food in front of the dog's nose if this helps to slow him.

Watch your dog as you prepare to stop. If you see him start to sit, take another step or two forward. When he is standing, immediately say "good stand" and reward with food. (Food is better than a toy for rewarding this behavior because a toy will excite the dog.)

After a few sessions like this, the dog begins to understand that the reward comes *only* when he's not moving and after the command to stand. Now you can actually take a slow, deliberate step away from the dog or slightly to the side. Then go back and reward him.

Next, start to move around the dog more. As long as he stands still, he can be rewarded from any angle. Once he realizes the reward comes when he's standing still, you can begin to shape the training sessions to be more like the actual exercise. Start picking up your speed, gradually going from a slow heel to a normal walking pace to running. This should be done over several training sessions. The most common mistake is trying to move along too quickly.

Recalls from the running stand should only be practiced every fourth time or so. Otherwise, the dog may begin to move forward because he is anticipating the recall.

When the dog does make a mistake and takes a step or two forward, correct with a verbal "no" or "eh, eh, eh"—whatever the dog knows as his correction—and start again. If the dog defies your command or is distracted, you may also have to give a leash correction. The level of physical and verbal correction needs to be based on the excitability and sensitivity of your dog.

The Recall

In the recall there are three factors that will affect your score: speed, the dog's front and the finish. The finish is always taught separately at the beginning. The correct front position is taught separately from the fast recall when the dog has a problem with either of these two elements. This is because one problem will always have an effect on the other. For instance, if you are emphasizing the correct front position, the dog may slow down. If he does and you reward him, you are reinforcing the slow return.

Our favorite way of teaching the recall with speed takes advantage of the dog's desire to play with the handler. Place the dog on a sit- or down-stay. (He must know the stay command to teach the recall this way.) Show him his toy and let the tension build. Don't call him immediately; wait until he is in extreme play drive and then call him to come. The goal is to reward speed here, so only do this three or four times. You need to judge how much energy the dog has to offer, and always end on a high note.

Another way of building up drive in order to increase speed is by having a second trainer hold the dog back by the collar while you run away from the dog, calling his name and generally exciting him.

There are many exercises you can do to improve your fronts. The easiest way to work on the front is to lure the dog into the correct position with food. You can spread your legs slightly to help the dog target the right spot. If the dog tends to err toward the left or right, you can position yourself so there is a fence or wall on that side. To see if the dog knows the correct position, you can turn slightly to one side so that he has to make the extra effort to go around and in front of you to get his reward.

The finish is taught with the same leash technique used to teach the dog to avoid crowding when heeling. The method is explained earlier in this chapter. It is a useful technique for showing the dog how to position his body.

The Retrieve

Teaching a dog to retrieve a dumbbell is an interesting and sometimes even controversial subject. Opinions differ greatly on how to train the retrieve, but *reliability* is a word that always comes up. Citing the need for overall reliability from the dog, many Schutzhund trainers believe force is necessary. Other trainers want to use the dog's natural drives and willingness. And still others use a combination of both.

The idea behind using force is that it is necessary to make the dog understand that refusing a command is not an option. Usually the force-retrieve is taught when the dog is just reaching his maturity. This is a time when the command can be useful in clearing up any ranking problem between the dog and the handler. The retrieve is a command that, when used regularly, will keep the rank order of the two clear.

The idea behind using the dog's natural drives is that the dog will happily take and retrieve the dumbbell as long as he has the right drives and is conditioned to the exercise all his life. In response to the question of reliability, these trainers say positive motivation is sufficient because there really aren't any significant distractions in a Schutzhund trial.

Depending on the dog, either method can get the job done. In general, what is important here is that the dog understands he *has to* do it. Retrieving something on command, regardless of the desire the dog may have to do so at the moment, is a subordinate act.

The philosophy we choose is squarely in the middle. We rely on the natural drives of the dog, but we teach the "forced hold" as a separate exercise from play retrieve, using a different dumbbell. We may use collar corrections from time to time, but it is the repetition that teaches the dog the exercise.

We choose the retrieving exercise to establish pack leadership over the dog. The Schutzhund dog is raised to be an assertive, self-confident dog. At some point in his life he needs to understand that he *has to* work for you, even if he doesn't feel like it. Establishing rank here will transfer to all other commands and help make it clear that you are the leader of the pack. He might be distracted or bored, but *quitting isn't an option!*

In teaching the retrieve, we thump the dog under the jaw for dropping or spitting out the dumbbell. Separately, we build drive with games of toss and fetch, but always with items other than the dumbbell. Using this approach, you will not need to put pressure on the dog to pick up the dumbbell (using the command "take it"), which could hurt his speed and desire. With proper training, the "take it" command won't be an issue you will fight over, since the dog has enjoyed the retrieve as a game all his life.

TEACHING THE RETRIEVE

As with any good training process, you must break down the exercise into smaller segments. This will help keep the dog from becoming stressed due to confusion, conflict or simply distraction. One of the main points to remember about retrieving is that it is a complex exercise. We will therefore review the training process as it begins and the segments as we teach them.

Step 1: Retrieving

From the time the dog is a puppy, retrieving things should be a big part of his life. Many different items can be retrieved: balls, Frisbees, hats, etc. At this stage, the dumbbell should not be used for the retrieving game. The act of retrieving and the fun of playing this game with you are the focus.

Step 2: Holding (9 to 16 Months Old)

This step should be done when the dog begins to mature but before he is old enough and big enough to overpower you. This is true for both mental and physical reasons.

Start with a small, plastic AKC-style dumbbell that is smaller than a Schutzhund dumbbell. With the dog sitting in the heel position, calmly insert the dumbbell into the dog's mouth with a minimum of fuss and hold his muzzle lightly but firmly with two hands. Make sure the dog's lips are not pinched under the dumbbell. After holding for just a few seconds, command the dog to "out," remove the dumbbell and reward him with food. You need several short sessions like this, building the holding time very slowly.

Working on the hold.
(Nanette Nickherson)

It is important *not to play fetch* with this same dumbbell. The dog needs to understand that simply *holding* the dumbbell results in reward. In fact, this dumbbell should seem boring to the dog. This keeps him from being anxious and chewing on the dumbbell. To make the dumbbell appear boring, you can show it to the dog and drop it as if you don't care about it. If the dog picks it up to solicit play from you, turn your back and ignore him. You can give the dumbbell a halfhearted kick as if to indicate its lack of importance—anything that will communicate disinterest to the dog.

When practicing the "hold" command with your dog, remember to cup his muzzle *lightly* in your hand. There should be no harshness in your grip. You must convey a quiet yet serious demeanor. Food rewards should always be there, but do not allow the dog to drop the dumbbell for the food. He must understand that *you* will give him the food *only* when he is not resisting keeping the dumbbell in his mouth.

When the dog understands that he must hold the dumbbell, it's time to teach him to sit in front of you. This is a more stressful position for the dog to be in. However, since he already knows the exercise, the stress should be minimal. After practicing the routine for a few more sessions from this position, you will be ready to continue. Now you can remove one hand from his muzzle and hold it lightly under his jaw, using the same reward system.

If the dog drops the dumbbell, thump the dog under the chin while using your correction word "eh, eh, eh!" or "no!" Never use this thump correction when the dumbbell is still in the dog's mouth. There should be no emotion with this correction, nor should the intensity of the correction be increased. The dog doesn't get it yet, and the correction is just to help him understand what you require.

All other corrections (for the dog moving or any other problem) should be done with the leash. You want to avoid pushing the dog into avoidance behavior. To ask for instant learning will only make him over-reactive. When the dog holds the dumbbell by himself for even five seconds, command "out," take the dumbbell and praise and reward him lavishly.

You also need to teach him to hold on tight. The dog should not chew, play with or balance the dumbbell loosely with his teeth. If he does, *bump it* out of his mouth with your hand and thump him under the chin with the other hand. The size and material of the plastic AKC dumbbell allows you to easily bump it out.

The left hand is touching the dumbbell while the right hand is ready to correct if the dog drops it.

The dog will soon learn that he is being set up. He will realize that he has to hang on tightly in order not to lose the dumbbell, just as if another dog were trying to steal his toy. The best part about this is that *the dog* will decide to do this. He doesn't have to be forced.

You may build up the holding time from this point. It may take up to six sessions, no longer than 10 minutes each, for the dog to hold the dumbbell firmly without help from you. You can proof or test the dog by offering him food while he has the dumbbell. If he drops the dumbbell, correct as before.

Step 3: Carrying the Dumbbell

When the dog is willing to accept, hold and release the dumbbell on your command, whether in the heel position or from a sit with you in front, you can begin to put him in motion with the dumbbell.

It is very likely that when you begin to move, the dog will spit out the dumbbell. So far all he knows is that he must hold the dumbbell when he's not moving. To teach him that he must also hold it as he heels, lightly hold the dog's muzzle, invite him to take a step or two and then reward. One or two steps at a time are okay, and don't let him make a mistake. *Every step of the way, you must plan on making the dog successful.*

If you must hold the dog's collar or keep him on a tight leash to get him to walk, make sure one hand is under his chin or touching his chest or neck, in case he tries to drop the dumbbell. If he does (and he will), don't make a big deal out of it and don't quit. Just put it back in his mouth and do the exercise long enough so that you can reward him. This is true even if you have to go back to the static sit.

Step 4: Carrying and Releasing

Now you can put two steps together. Place the dumbbell in the dog's mouth and have him heel. When you stop, he should sit automatically without dropping the dumbbell. He should keep holding it as you start walking with him heeling again. At the end of this exercise, you may step in front of him and command "out" as he releases the dumbbell, just as he would in a trial.

Step 5: Distractions

When the dog knows the entire retrieve exercise, you can begin to add distractions—first with food and then with a toy. Move the food over his head, to the side of his head and eventually put it on the end of the dumbbell. The dog should hold fast to the dumbbell. If he lets go, he should be corrected. You should always be ready with one hand under his chin. As the distractions progress, you should be able to begin heeling with distractions.

Step 6: Introducing the Schutzhund Dumbbell

We have spoken about separating the "hold" exercise from the fun retrieving exercise. Now you can put the dog in *complete rest* for a few days (no training and no play), so that when he is brought out he will show more drive than normal.

Now it's time to bring out the Schutzhund dumbbell and excite the dog with it as you would a toy, then throw it five or six feet from you. The dog should be on a long line so he cannot run off with the dumbbell.

Using the favorite tug toy as a distraction.

Do not use the line or put tension on it unless it's necessary. There is no negative association with this dumbbell because you have been practicing with a different type of dumbbell for the hold command, and you should try to keep it that way.

Let the dog take the dumbbell, then call him to you. Depending on how calm the dog is, you may ask him to sit in front of you and then give the command "hold," or walk slowly backward in a circle while commanding "hold" until you finally stop and tell him to sit and hold.

If the dog drops it, again give a light thump under the chin and place the dumbbell in his mouth. Then do a quick "out" and lots of praise and reward (food). You don't want to use a toy reward at this point, as it will diminish the importance of the dumbbell.

Once you get two or three successful retrieves, end the session on a high note. Again, make the dog rest. Later that day, try for the same success. If you have trouble, go back to the part of the training where you think the trouble began. When things are going smoothly, you may begin to build the distance of your toss.

Introducing the Schutzhund dumbbell.

Do's and Don'ts for the Retrieve

1. Be sure that you have already established a bond with the dog before teaching the retrieve.

2. All corrections should be matter-of-fact, and not overdone. The moment the dog drops the dumbbell, he gets corrected. Pick up the dumbbell calmly (don't rush and spook the dog) and continue on.

3. If the dog fights you when you're placing the dumbbell in his mouth, you were probably too sharp on a correction. Use your fingers around the top of the dog's muzzle to open his jaw, insert your fingers and then the dumbbell. Make sure the food reward is always present in order to offer the dog motivation.

4. Always lift the dog's lips and double-check to make sure they have not been caught between the dumbbell and his teeth. Make sure the dog's jowls don't fold under, causing him to bite down on the skin at the same time as the dumbbell. This can cause pain related to the dumbbell.

5. Allow the dog some breaks between sessions so he doesn't get too nervous.

6. In the beginning, do not try to maintain the "hold" command for long. The time should be just long enough for you to touch both sides of the dumbbell, remove your hands and then "out" and release.

7. When the dog pretends to hold the dumbbell and is just balancing it, knock it out of his mouth and give him a thump under the chin with a verbal correction.

8. Never give a correction when the dumbbell is in the dog's mouth.

Common Problems with the Retrieve

Chewing the Dumbbell

The most common problem is the dog chewing on the dumbbell. Some trainers will be happy to accept a less firm grip on the dumbbell if they can eliminate the chewing. However, a dog that doesn't grip the dumbbell firmly is more likely to drop it. Therefore, trainers have experimented over the last century with ways to keep the dog from chewing and ways to tighten the grip. Some of the ideas they've come up with include:

1. Wrap copper wire around the dowel of the dumbbell to discourage the dog from chewing it.
2. Drill a hole into one side of the dumbbell and fill it with lead. This will make the dumbbell lopsided and force the dog to hang onto it tightly.
3. Tie a line to one end of the dumbbell and keep it moving. This is similar to working with a tug. The idea is to make the dumbbell move like prey. When the dog catches the dumbbell, he has to hold on for a tug game. If he loosens his grip, he will lose the dumbbell and have to give chase again. The dog may learn to keep a good grip on the dumbbell from this exercise. But be aware that some dogs may learn to think of the dumbbell as a toy and therefore may chew it when it's not on the line.
4. Instead of the dumbbell, use a dowel without the ends, attached to a string, so that when you pull it, the dowel will slide from the dog's mouth if he doesn't grip it. Wait for a good grip, and then "out" and reward.

These are all gimmicks, and they all can work. Everything being equal, we still prefer to teach the "hold" command as a discipline exercise.

Slow on the Return

If this is your dog's problem, make sure to train this when the dog has plenty of energy. Some dogs will never be speedy retrievers simply because of their breed or genetic characteristics. It is important to recognize your dog's potential and his faults, and to keep your expectations reasonable.

Make the retrieve fun, and set aside a special time to train it, rather than making it part of a routine that includes a lot of other exercises. This can really help improve the dog's speed. Then do several sessions of obedience exercises without any retrieves, and you'll make the dog want to retrieve more. Do not do anything related to play for a while, and when you go back to the retrieve, the dog's speed will pick up. Gradually start to ask for other commands a little at a time as you see the speed pick up.

Speed can also be increased by passing up the flat retrieve for a while. When your dog jumps the A-frame, he will need to pick up some speed in order to make the jump. Because of this, he will end up in front of you almost immediately on the return. If you reward him immediately, he will learn that the faster he gets to you, the quicker the reward.

When you *are* working on the flat, try moving your position to the left or right while the dog is moving away. When the dog turns back and has to look for you, he may focus harder on you next time and therefore pick up some speed.

Using backward movement and a long line to correct a lazy dog will work sometimes, but the dog can easily come to rely on these aids. The use of a long line can also hinder a dog so much that he may refuse to retrieve at all.

Jumping Problems

We always advise that hip and elbow X-rays be taken before asking any dog to jump at trial heights. This is to ensure that the dog is free of pain while jumping. If you have a breed that is prone to back problems, or suspect an ailment or injury, an X-ray of the back may also be in order. *Never* ask a dog to jump if he is physically incapable of doing so pain-free.

You always want to start a dog on low jumps and work your way up. If, after a few sessions, the dog is clearing the jump but is still lazy and is pushing the top off, put a PVC pipe on top. When the dog pushes off, the pipe will fall to the ground, startling him. Do not reward such a jump. Next time, the dog will try harder not to knock down the pipe. When the pipe does not fall, reward the dog lavishly. Using a toy reward works best in most cases. Soon the connection will be made.

Next, make the dog jump in both directions before he is rewarded. Gradually increase the height, but be patient and go slowly. A one-meter jump should never be a problem for a healthy working dog. The problem is usually a handler who pushes the dog too fast, too high and too soon. Don't rush to pair the dumbbell with the jump until both are well established as separate exercises.

Another important factor in jumping is where the dog is positioned in front of the jump. Like any athlete—human, horse or dog—there must be a comfortable distance between the athlete and the jump. The proper distance depends on the dog. For some dogs, 10 feet is necessary;

This style of jumping may look good, but it will cost points and may result in injury. (Doug Loving)

for others only five. It is up to you to watch carefully and see what is the best distance. This is also true for the distance you will throw the dumbbell.

Exposure to all kinds of jumps—A-frames, solid, bushes, bars, etc.—helps the dog become confident.

On the A-frame, the biggest problem is the dog jumping off the top rather than climbing down. Start with the A-frame at a very low height. Make the dog walk over it a few times. Gradually increase the height while walking the dog over it.

If this is still a problem, stand close to the side of the A-frame and drop the dumbbell not far from the backside. This helps the dog come straight down instead of leaping off the top. Another trick is to place two chairs seven to ten feet from the A-frame, so that when the dog is coming back over the obstacle he is cautious when coming down.

The Send Away

Assuming the dog already responds well to the "down" command, you can start training the send away. The exercise is divided into two parts: the go out and the down. Psychologically, the go out should be related to getting the toy, and the down related to obedience.

To make your dog go fast in a full-out run straight down the field, use a toy as a reward. When you first start teaching this exercise, you will want the dog to see the object of his desire. As long as the dog can see the object, he will go straight to it rather than slowing to sniff and look for it. Later, you will want to teach him to trust that it will "magically" appear as long as he obeys the command.

With a long line on the dog, start at a distance of 15 feet so that the dog can go and get the object without making a mistake. To get the dog charged for the toy, a pre-cue ("Where's your toy?") can be given. In a trial this is not cheating, as you are not yet being judged. It creates focus on the assignment, which helps you and your dog complete the exercise successfully.

In training the send away, once the dog knows "go out" means "get your toy," you're ready to introduce the "down" command. Some preliminary work can be done by the way you play with the dog. Bring the dog into drive by teasing him with the toy. Then pretend that you're throwing the toy, and as the dog takes off, command "down." On the first few tries it may take him some time to comply, but he'll quickly understand that sometimes he has to lie down if he wants the toy to be thrown for him.

Next, place the toy at a distance and give the down command almost as soon as the dog is sent for it. This is so the dog does not associate the down with the toy. As soon as he lies down, the reward will be the command "go out" again—and this time he will go to the toy and play as a reward.

As soon as the dog seems to understand that sending him for the reward can be interrupted and is complying willingly, you can move to the next step, which is increasing the distance. The first few times, most likely the dog will not lie down. At this point, do *not* play with him. This is when you use the long line. Reel the dog in and, if he has taken the toy, take it from him. This is all without great drama or chase games. Then put the toy back where you want it.

Next, start to give the down command closer to the toy (almost right in front of it), always having him wait for the command "take it." This exercise requires both speed and precise discipline.

COMMON PROBLEMS WITH THE SEND AWAY

The most common problems handlers run into are going out slow and not lying down. When you teach the down, it is important to start with short distances. The dog must learn that "go out" may sometimes be interrupted by the down command. He must accept this fact and feel confident that he will still be rewarded if he follows the commands. The dog must also understand that the interruption (down command) will happen *only* when the handler decides. The dog should not be given the opportunity to anticipate the down. This is why the down command is given periodically and in no particular pattern, so that the dog does not begin to generalize.

Just as in all training, timing in this exercise is of the utmost importance. During the initial stages of training, as soon as the dog lies down correctly, even reluctantly, the reward should be as instantaneous as possible. Make sure the dog's elbows are on the ground before you reward him. This may take a few more seconds to establish, but it is very important that the object of the exercise be clear in the dog's mind. You don't want a dog that hovers with his elbows off the ground as he anticipates the reward. If this part of the exercise is rushed, it can create conflict and confusion later.

Now you can start teaching the dog directions. Use a hand signal to indicate where you want the dog to go. Unfortunately, most dogs think of this signal as a "go" signal rather than a directional indicator. To make sure your dog understands what you want, place two toys at 90-degree angles. Send him after just one, using the directional hand signal. This helps to teach the dog that he can only go out after the toy that the hand signal indicates. Because he knows there are two choices and only the one being indicated by the hand signal is acceptable, he learns the hand signal means "go there" and not just "go."

According to the rules of competition, the hand signal must be held. As the dog lies down, the hand may go down. This indicates the exercise is completed.

Another way to teach direction is to use a well-planted orchard. Staying in the middle of the rows of trees, send the dog out several times, in all four directions. The rows of trees will help the dog run straight. Use the hand signal only for direction, and reward with a toy as you normally would.

When you start increasing the distance, you may want to elevate the toy temporarily. Use something to lift the toy off the ground a bit, but not something too obvious. A small thermos or box, perhaps, but don't hang it from a pole or something that would make it look unusual.

Again, at a greater distance you will want to have some "free" send outs where the dog does not receive a down command. This is to keep him moving quickly down the field and not kill off his drive. The result of too many down commands will be that he will anticipate them and slow down. That's why you must make an effort to keep from being predictable.

Another way to get a quick response is to let the dog know when he goes out quickly and downs that you, in turn, will run quickly to him to reward. Your dog knows when you are making an effort. If you run down the field and release him to play tug or release him while tossing a ball, you will reward his enthusiasm with your own.

After the dog understands this lesson, you can add the sit. This completes the exercise. Again, vary what the dog does before each release. Sometimes reward after the go out and down, sometimes after the send part and other times after the complete exercise.

The next step is teaching the dog to *believe* you. This means convincing him that when you say "down," you know where the ball is 100 percent of the time. "Magically," the ball or toy appears. You do this by a sleight of hand: getting the dog to turn his attention in one direction while dropping the toy behind his back from the other. He will begin to understand that the reward will always be where you say. Later, the dog will inevitably realize that you've been tricking him, but by this time the behavior will already be established. You will no longer need to place the toy at the other end of the field.

Because of the desire and drive necessary for this exercise, you should not practice it too many times in one session. You do not want to risk the dog slowing down. This is especially true after the exercise is understood and established. Boredom is unlikely in the beginning of the training because the distances are short and the exercise is new. But as the newness wears off, boredom can set in.

A good way to keep all of the exercises from becoming monotonous is to make each training session end with a jackpot. This is a play reward that goes on for a long time. You may do just one send away and end with a jackpot. The next day, you may do a send away and heel exercise and end with a jackpot. This way the dog never knows what will happen and is always up and eager.

The Pattern in Obedience

Some trainers prefer to go through the whole sequence of exercises (heel, sit, down and so on) during training in the same way they would in a trial. We find that dogs trained by going through the routine this way show good results at first, but after more sessions they start to anticipate too much and have to be corrected more often for anticipating a command than for not obeying it. We prefer to mix up the order of the exercises or work on only a few per session.

Going to a different club for practice is also a must if you want to do well in the sport. This way, the dog does not become conditioned to perform only on your home field. Frequently changing the direction we work the send aways and the heeling patterns will also help avoid this kind of conditioning. Simply start each training session from a different point on the field. A dog worked this way will perform much better on an unfamiliar field.

Most dogs need to practice the send away on a new field at least once. In most cases, a dog that comes out fresh onto a new field will have some difficulty in going straight. This may be because a new direction is required (southeast or northwest, for example). One thing that seems to help is heeling the dog in a straight line in the direction in which you will send him. When you move up and back on the field in the direction you want him to go, it helps him generalize the direction.

Physical Correction

Although our training methods are based on positive motivation and withholding the reward, there still may be a need for physical correction to complete the learning and create the proper relationship and balance with the dog. Correction should *only* be used when you are *absolutely* sure the dog knows what you are asking from him.

For a correction to be effective, it must be

1. Immediate
2. Strong enough to suppress the unwanted behavior
3. Associated only with the unwanted behavior
4. Occur every time the unwanted behavior occurs

We use physical correction for two different reasons and in two different ways. The first reason is for a distraction that causes the dog to stop paying attention and simply not hear you. When this happens, take care that the command given is not associated with the correction. Rather, it should be associated with the distraction. The dog is not openly defying you; he is preoccupied with something else. The last thing you want to do is make him overly worried about the command. The command wasn't the problem anyway.

To correct a distraction, give two or three quick jerks on the training collar while the dog is distracted. Do *not* repeat the command and do not push him into the desired position because this will make the dog associate the correction with the command.

The second reason for a correction is when a dog does not obey the actual command—although we are selective about when to use a physical correction for this behavior. One situation where we would physically correct a dog for not obeying is when he is asked to sit in a place where there is some water on the ground. The correction doesn't have to be very forceful, but the dog does have to understand that he doesn't have a choice. You have no idea what the conditions will be at a trial, and once the dog knows it is possible to defy a command, he's likely to try it again.

In this situation, repeat the command and give the dog two or three quick jerks on the training collar. Direct your collar correction so that it forces him into the desired position.

THE RIGHT COLLAR

Collars will vary from dog to dog and handler to handler—from fur-savers, standard chokers and prong (also called pinch) collars. You need to decide which one you want to use, based on your dog's response to corrections. The most important thing to remember is not to use a collar that is more severe than the dog requires. This can only lead to bad results.

It's really not necessary to keep switching collars once you find the appropriate collar for your dog. The concern is that if a prong collar works best, come trial time when the dog is wearing a fur-saver, he will not behave properly. Stay with the collar that enables you to use minimal physical effort to get the response you need. This way, you won't have to use it too often in training to condition the behavior in the dog. By trial time it will be unimportant what collar the dog is wearing.

The Schutzhund III
Protection Test

Properly assessing protection work is of the utmost importance in selecting working dogs for breeding purposes. For this reason, the assessment of the protection work must have the highest priority. The protection test is especially effective in differentiating natural performance attributes from learned ones.

Some of the most important criteria for assessing a dog include:

- Ability to withstand pressure
- Self-assuredness
- Steady nerves
- Balanced drives
- Natural protective behavior
- Willingness to take direction (follow commands)

The protection test at this advanced level plays out an elaborate drama in which a helper, acting as the bad guy, is found by the dog, is searched by the handler, escapes, is apprehended and escorted, attacks both dog and handler, escapes again and is reapprehended. The dog must display exceptional courage and fighting instincts, along with supreme control. A dog with a brave heart can thrill all who watch with his protection work.

Revier or Search for the Helper

THE HELPER

- The helper is placed in a designated blind while the dog and handler are out of sight.
- The helper must be placed in such a way that the dog will have to search five blinds, back and forth across the imaginary center line of the training field (the midline), before finding the helper in the sixth blind.

THE HANDLER

- The handler should walk down the midline during the exercise.
- The handler must call the dog back after each search and direct him to search the blind on the opposite side of the field.
- The dog's call name can be used with the search command.

THE DOG

- The dog should quickly move away from the handler when he hears the command and sees the appropriate hand signal. He should go straight to the directed blind.
- The dog should search intensively and thoroughly.
- When commanded by the handler to come back and search in another direction, the dog should quickly and immediately do so.

Hold and Bark

THE HELPER

- The helper shall stop all movement when the dog finds him.
- Upon the handler's request, the helper will step out of the blind.

- The helper should stand still while the handler searches him.

THE HANDLER

- As soon as the dog reaches the helper, the handler should stop. At the judge's request, the handler will approach to within four paces of the blind.
- When the judge requests, the handler will recall the dog and then order the helper to step out from the blind.
- The handler will command the dog into a down position in the area designated by the judge. Then the handler will search the helper for weapons and search the blind for discarded objects.

THE DOG

- When the dog reaches the helper, he must bark aggressively and continuously, but without touching the helper. The guarding has to be persistent right up to the call-out. The dog must be sure of himself.
- The dog must come quickly into the heel position when ordered by the handler.
- The dog must lie down in front of the helper on command and remain there as the handler searches.

Escape and Defense

THE HELPER

- When directed by the judge, the helper should attempt to escape by running away from the dog.
- When the dog bites the sleeve, the helper tries to pull away for a few steps and then freezes if the dog maintains his grip.
- When the judge directs, the helper will attack the dog using the flexible stick as a defensive weapon, but not striking the dog at first. When the dog has gripped the helper firmly, the helper will strike the dog twice on nonvital parts of the body with the flexible stick.

THE HANDLER

- At the judge's request, the handler will step up to the dog and helper after the escape and defense.
- The handler will not take the stick from the helper.

THE DOG

- The dog must stop the helper's attempted escape by biting the sleeve with a firm grip, and then hold the helper in place with spellbound attention.
- When the helper stops trying to escape, the dog must release the helper automatically or on command from his handler, and then guard the helper, allowing no further movement.
- When the helper moves to attack the dog again, he must immediately counter the attack, with a full and firm grip on the sleeve. When the dog is hit by the stick, he must not let go of the sleeve or loosen his grip.

A'Shane Ot Vitosha, SchHIII, IPOIII, at the 1998 USA Nationals, where he earned 100 points in protection.

Back Transport

THE HELPER

- The helper will be transported approximately 40 paces through a series of turns, as specified by the judge.
- The helper must conceal the stick during the transport so that it will be a surprise when the helper uses it later to attack the handler.

THE HANDLER

- The handler will order the dog to heel and direct the helper to move forward.
- The handler and the dog follow at approximately five paces behind.

THE DOG

- When he is commanded to heel, the dog will move into position at the handler's left side and follow the helper at a distance of five paces.
- The dog should remain alert to the helper and responsive to the handler.

Defense Against Attack

THE HELPER

- During the transport, the helper will attack the handler on the judge's signal. After being counterattacked by the dog, the helper will press the dog and try to push him away. The helper ceases the fight upon the judge's signal. He will then be side transported to the judge.

THE HANDLER

- After being attacked by the helper during the transport, the handler will disarm the helper and escort him to the judge by side transport.

THE DOG

- When the handler is attacked by the helper, the dog should stop the attack with an energetic grip. The dog should then side transport the helper and exit the field with the handler in a free-heeling position.

Defense Against Attack and Guarding the Helper, Defense Against Re-Attack

THE HELPER

- A second helper will move into a blind designated by the judge, at a distance of 70 to 80 paces. At the judge's request, the helper will leave the blind and, after the handler issues a command to stop, will ignore the instruction and begin a frontal attack upon the handler and the dog.
- The helper will stand still on the judge's signal, after the dog has apprehended him with a firm grip.
- At the judge's direction, the helper will attack the dog again using the flexible stick. The helper will again strike the dog twice on nonvital areas. After the hits, the helper will cease the aggression.
- The helper will be disarmed by the handler and side transported for about 40 paces. The helper should watch the dog without assuming a threatening posture or making any defensive movements.
- It is not necessary for the helper to remain absolutely motion-less. The helper must protect their body with the protective sleeve and remain quiet whenever the dog is holding them with gaze and body position.

THE HANDLER

- At the judge's request, the handler will heel his dog to a blind designated by the judge. The dog must sit by the handler's side and remain calm and attentive to the helper, until released by a command. Upon seeing the helper emerge from the blind, the handler will order the helper to stop.

- The handler will release the dog to pursue the helper, who ignores the command to stop. The handler is permitted to follow up to a distance of 40 paces.
- After the helper attacks the dog, the handler will remain for about 30 seconds without influencing the dog. Upon direction from the judge, the handler will proceed to the dog and disarm the helper.
- The handler and dog will side transport the helper to the judge. The handler will then leave the field with the free-heeling dog.

THE DOG

- The dog will free-heel to the designated blind and sit by his handler's side. He should remain calm but focused on the helper.
- Upon command from the handler, the dog will counterattack the helper as the helper flees down the field. The dog must use the shortest possible route.

Ivan Balabanov and Bocca Ot Vitosha, SchHIII, on the reattack after the courage test.

- The dog must not be influenced by the helper's attempts to intimidate him. The dog must not hesitate to attack the helper, and must hold the helper with a firm grip.
- The dog must let go of the helper when the helper ceases the aggression and stands quietly.
- The dog must again grip the helper firmly when they reattack and strike the dog with the stick, and again let go of the helper when they cease all aggression and stand quietly.
- The dog should side transport the helper back to the judge, and then leave the training field in a free-heeling position with his handler.

Scoring

The advanced protection test is scored this way:

Maximum Points	100 points
Revier, or search for the helper	5 points
Hold and bark	10 points
Escape	10 points
Defense	20 points
Back transport	5 points
Defense against attack	15 points
Defense against attack with on-watch position and guarding the helper	20 points
Defense against reattack	15 points

The dog's fighting instinct is analyzed by the judge during the entire protection test. In addition to a numerical score, the judge will rate the dog's courage and fighting instincts. They may be rated as Pronounced (*Ausgeprägt* in German), Sufficient (*Vorhanden*) or Insufficient (*Nicht Genügend*).

The way the dog presses toward the helper and the sureness of his grip on the sleeve are convincing signs of a developed fighting instinct. Should a dog avoid the stick hits, he must immediately become the aggressor again and independently engage the fight.

After the courage test, if the dog returns to the handler or remains in the vicinity of the helper without his attention being locked on the helper, then in the final analysis the dog cannot receive the evaluation

Different Rules

It's important to note that there are differences between the Schutzhund rules accepted by United Schutzhund Clubs of America and the international (IPO) rules. For example, when competing under IPO rules, after the dog is called from the hold and bark, the handler doesn't search the helper. Instead, the dog sits and the handler goes into the blind. When the helper tries to flee, the dog is not supposed to break the sit until he is released by the handler with a bite command. If the dog takes off on his own, as in Schutzhund USA rules, there is a major point deduction!

The rules change somewhat from year to year, and we advise you to keep up-to-date with all new rules accepted by the leading organizations.

Pronounced. This top rating can only be awarded to dogs with an especially developed, joyful fighting instinct.

Knowing when to stop fighting is equally important. Only the energetic fighting and firm-gripping dog that releases after one "out" command will receive a full score. The voice command to let go is permitted only once in each exercise. Dogs that let go only after bodily contact by the handler cannot pass the test.

There are also other reasons a dog may fail the protection test. Dogs that can be pressed away by the helper and dogs that fail any one fighting exercise cannot pass (the pursuit is considered a fighting exercise). After the dog has failed one fighting exercise, the protection phase must be discontinued.

A dog is also dismissed if he demonstrates temperament problems during the trial, even if the initial test was positive.

Tapping a Dog's Drives

The dictionary definition of drive is a force, an urge, a basic need, a compulsive energy. In protection training, when trainers refer to drives, most of the time they mean the relationship between predator and prey, maternal instincts, territorial instincts, and so on. Drives are innate and are important to the survival of any species.

Protection terminology was developed in the course of describing the dog's inborn traits and natural inherited tendencies. We use this terminology to describe, analyze and teach one another how to provoke a dog into reacting in a particular way.

In nature, the most likely outcome of a predator-prey confrontation is that the predator kills the prey. In dog training we make use of this same drive, although the dog does not actually have to kill anything. The helper takes their cues from nature, moving the way prey moves. This is what triggers the prey drive in the predator. Prey runs away, hides, sneaks, makes sudden movements and is generally afraid of the predator. These are all cues the helper can use to bring out the prey drive in the dog.

But in protection a dog doesn't (and shouldn't) always work through prey drive. During a fight with the helper, the dog is constantly switching between drives—as is the helper. Prey is usually afraid and tries to avoid confrontation with the predator, but when cornered, it may attempt to defend itself. This may cause the predator to switch temporarily into avoidance behavior, allowing just enough time for the prey to escape. So, even though we have prey and predator, they may, from time to time, switch roles. This is why it is so important for the helper to be able to recognize which drive the dog is working in and how they should respond.

PREY DRIVE

Prey drive is the one used most in protection training. When starting protection work, we always try to induce the dog to bite through his prey drive. This way the dog does not feel threatened and is comfortable trying to dominate the situation.

To promote prey drive, the helper has to show the dog that they are afraid of the dog. The helper presents the sleeve or the tug to the dog in a way that imitates a prey animal: moving from side to side, popping out from behind something, darting away quickly as if trying to hide and generally acting frightened.

When the dog bites, the helper's body language should also imitate prey: trying to escape, emitting high-pitched squeals and then relaxing as if giving up. If the dog begins to loosen up on the sleeve, the helper tries to escape just as prey would. This teaches the dog to keep a strong

Ivan works with Rosie von Euztal to build prey drive. (Debbie Dilley)

grip on the sleeve. This is best done with the dog in a harness, so the pressure is on the dog's chest rather than his neck.

For his finale, the prey will put on a big, final struggle to try to escape. The helper should also do this. The helper rewards the dog's persistence by slipping off the sleeve or tug. Let the dog run around the field with it and celebrate his win.

DEFENSE DRIVE

The defense drive is often used in combination with the prey drive. Working prey-driven dogs in defense drive will make them more balanced and serious.

When working the dog in defense, you are bringing out his instinct to protect himself. It is important that the helper does not overwhelm the dog when working him in defense drive. The dog must be pressured enough to react, but not so much that he goes into avoidance. Signs of a dog coming into defense are:

- Darting eye contact and choosing to either stare or avoid eye contact, depending on what works for the dog
- Trying to bite anything that is in his range and that he considers a threat

- Growling
- Showing teeth
- A fixed gaze
- General signs of worry

When we say that we work the dog in defense, we are not trying to make him *overly defensive*. We are trying to irritate him just enough to bring out intensity rather than play. Then we let him dominate and win the fight.

When we talk about defensive aggression, it is important to understand that the dog has four options available to him:

1. Initiate the fight and try to overpower the helper (this is the desired response).
2. Flee from danger.
3. Submit and try to make friends with the helper.
4. Ignore the situation and pretend it is not happening.

Some dogs work quite well in prey drive, but when pushed into defensive aggression, they choose an option that is not desirable for a Schutzhund dog. Some of the behaviors the dog may display to avoid confrontation are hiding behind the handler, trying to escape in a panicked fashion, making a play bow, holding his ears back, casting his eyes down, tucking his tail, lying down, rolling over, sniffing the ground or acting preoccupied with something else.

Which way the dog will respond depends on his natural level of defense drive, his maturity and his comfort level. These factors will determine which way we approach training. There are three possibilities:

1. A mature dog that can choose on his own to go into defense drive can be introduced to protection work in defense drive. The helper should be careful to balance provoking defensive aggression with prey movements. This will help develop the dog's fighting drive.
2. For the dog that is more comfortable with prey drive, we periodically mimic the prey fighting back as if cornered to call forth his defense drive. From a position where the prey "plays dead," the helper can briefly charge the dog and, in the end, let the dog win when the dog counters with defensive aggression of his own.

Encouraging the dog to work with his prey drive by using a line attached to the sleeve. (Debbie Dilley)

3. With the overly defensive dog, we want to bring out his prey drive. One way to do this is by putting the sleeve on the end of a line and dragging it in front of the dog. He gets to play tug-of-war, but when he loosens his grip, the sleeve is pulled away from him. He will learn to hold onto it tightly for fear that it will run away. This also makes it clearer in the dog's mind that the sleeve is what he's fighting for.

FIGHTING DRIVE

Your goal should be to develop a fighting drive as the dog matures through his training experience. The fighting drive is shown through the dog's desire to overpower and dominate his opponent.

The dog should win the fight through both the prey and defense drives, and it is out of these that the fighting drive grows. Aggression in a dog can be passive or active. Passive aggression includes the undesirable traits of defense drive. Active aggression comes from the desired traits of defense drive.

It's important to note that dogs that have fighting drive also have strong prey drive. This dog knows how to win the prey and how to protect his prize. The dog should always perceive the helper as a rival. The competition between dog and helper can be over prey or social dominance.

To develop fighting drive, the dog also needs to know how to defend himself from the helper. It is out of this learning combination that the dog becomes dominant and intimidates the helper through fighting drive.

Equipment for Protection Training

Training Collars
    Pinch collar: for a dog that needs strong corrections
    German steel choke: for a more sensitive dog
    Fur-saver collar: for a trained dog
    Leather collar: to cushion the neck; used with a long line
Harness: to prevent pressure on the neck; used with a long line
Back-tie: a nylon long line with a rubber strap; causes less pressure on the neck
Bungee line: a long line that creates a reflex action if the dog does not hold a good grip on the sleeve
Scratch pants: protective overalls made of leather or nylon to prevent leg injury from scratches or bites
Sleeve: puppy soft sleeve and intermediate trial sleeve
Sticks: padded leather stick, nylon Schlagstock, reed stick, nylon or leather popper with whip on end, bamboo clatter stick

TESTING DRIVES

In working the Schutzhund dog, you must know which drive the dog is in. This is important because you don't want the dog to do the work strictly as a game, with the sleeve as the ultimate toy.

To find out which drive the dog is in, put him on a long line. The helper can agitate him and then throw the sleeve down to the side. This should be done far enough away that the dog cannot grab the sleeve. If the dog ignores the helper and focuses on the sleeve, he is working too much in prey drive and this needs to be corrected. The helper should

Bocca Ot Vitosha, SchHIII, and David Delessagas are working in fighting drive. (Nanette Nickherson)

then make sure to psychologically present himself or herself as more of a direct threat to the dog. The helper should wait until the dog comes at him or her with direct eye contact before giving the dog the sleeve. A hidden sleeve or full-body suit can also help make the dog take the helper more seriously.

If the dog ignores the sleeve and focuses only on the helper, he is working too much in defense drive.

Ideally, when the helper throws down the sleeve, the dog should go back and forth between the sleeve and the helper. The dog should not be fixed on either. This means the dog understands that the sleeve is important, but also that the helper must go and get it before the fight can start.

Early Development of a Schutzhund Dog

When can you start to protection train your dog? This question has been much debated throughout the years. The answer is right away, as long as you keep in mind the fact that all puppies are different.

Kathy O'Brien's Dynomite Ot Vitosha at four months old.

In general, you can use play to ignite the prey drive, but you will not be working much with defense until the pup is mature—12 to 18 months old. Although we personally like to start at a young age, there is really no right or wrong answer. Much will be determined by the style of training you are using.

PRELIMINARY WORK

Protection training, just like other forms of training, should be done in the proper sequence, taking into consideration what the dog has to offer at any particular point in time. For example, a dog that is still gaining confidence and skills in basic bite work should not be asked to perform a courage test. This will only create problems and inconsistencies in the dog's work.

There is a delicate balancing act that goes on in the preliminary stages of training. Dogs that are handler-sensitive and tend to submit easily to discipline in the obedience phase often do not show enough

We're building a dog's confidence by making it really obvious who is stronger. This is Sammie and Rosie. (Debbie Dilley)

intensity to move through the protection exercises without displaying weakness or avoidance behavior. On the other hand, dogs that are extremely intense in protection work are difficult to bring under control in the obedience portions of the work.

Many control problems can develop from the fight. These include avoiding the handler, redirected aggression (toward the handler) or taking cheap shots (being incorrect in the bite work) due to frustration.

INTRODUCING THE STICK

We like to introduce the stick (as well as other items that may distract or concern the dog) when the dog is young. You can use a plastic soda or water bottle or other novel item in a nonthreatening manner with the young dog or pup. Let the dog see and touch the object first, then rub it on the dog gently. All of this builds confidence.

When first introducing whips and Schlagstocks, crack the whip well away from the young dog while giving him the puppy sleeve as a reward.

When you've worked at conditioning the pup and he no longer acknowledges the stick or gives it a second thought, you are ready to

Introducing a plastic stick to Jeff's three-month-old puppy, Finnegan. (LiLiana Varbonov)

It's very important during protection training for the dog to have a clear understanding of when the fight is over and who won! (Martha Hoffman)

move on. Have the dog actually go through the stick in order to get to the sleeve. This is done while the dog is on a long line. Present the sleeve but intentionally make him miss, keeping the stick below the sleeve. Using a motion that focuses the dog's attention on the sleeve, touch him on the chest with the stick as he comes in for the bite. As soon as he reaches the target, release the sleeve. Thus, he gains confidence that the stick is not so significant or dangerous.

THE IMPORTANCE OF AN EXPERIENCED HELPER

There is nothing more important to the success of your training in the protection exercises than to have an experienced helper. It is this person's function to react to the dog with the exact timing that is necessary to elicit the best possible responses. Many of the movements the helper will make are subtle. This body language can be so subtle, in fact, that an untrained eye would not even notice. But a dog always will.

The experienced helper understands when a dog needs to be pressed harder, when he is overly stressed and needs a release, when he needs to be excited and when he needs soothing. A good helper will teach the dog to initiate the fight and be the active one, instead of offering lots of movements, encouragement and treats—which will teach the dog to simply react to the helper's actions. The good helper can play a dog emotionally, the way a good musician plays an instrument.

Body Language

Some of the ways a helper can use his body include:

Pressing the Dog	Relieving Pressure
Eye contact	Lack of eye contact
Full frontal view of the body	Side view of the body
Hovering over the dog	Crouching down and away from the dog
Yelling and waving the stick	Running away

Andre Vandergeten works with Boril Ot Vitosha, SchHII. (Ivan Balabanov)

In addition to body language, a helper needs to know how and when to properly present a bite to the dog, how and when to cease movement in order to keep the dog from gaining a reward, how to place stick hits, how to read the dog's body language, when to change drives and when to heighten or relieve the pressure. These are just *a few* of the things a good helper needs to know.

Problem Solving in Advanced Protection

Perhaps the most obvious problem in Schutzhund is the dog that doesn't want to bite. A dog that lets go of the sleeve during the bite, or will not bite at all, may not have the confidence or the fighting drive from the beginning. Some dogs will make a reasonable effort the first few times the sleeve is presented. However, when it becomes apparent that they will need to sustain the bite and fight with the helper, these dogs are just not up to it. It is not fair to try to force such a dog to do the work.

We would like to make it clear that *not every dog can make a good Schutzhund prospect.* If your dog does not choose to be a Schutzhund dog, you should not force it. Heart and desire are things a dog is born with. You cannot train them.

If your dog loves everything but the protection phase, you might consider doing just the obedience and tracking tests (currently offered by DVG).

Bad Bites on the Sleeve

Letting go of the sleeve, chewing on the sleeve, targeting the end of the sleeve and biting with the front of the mouth are all problems we try to improve in training. The full mouth bite is not the only criterion by which the dog is judged. The way the dog fights, hangs on the sleeve (showing sureness) or growls while biting (showing unsureness) are all judged.

Lack of experience can cause any of these problems. The dog may be tentative the first few times he bites. He may bump the sleeve or spit it out if it is made of different material than he is used to or if it is harder or softer. Repetition should eliminate this problem, as long as you have a good helper.

Bad teeth can be another problem. Some dogs have a genetic predisposition to tooth and gum problems. Teeth can be painful, loose in the gums or brittle, and they may break easily. If the dog shows a strong desire to bite and goes into the bite hard, yet spits out the sleeve unexpectedly, this could be the reason.

Structural problems in the back, hips, elbows or knees can also account for slipping off the sleeve. Sometimes a dog will have all of the drive necessary for the work, but the fight with the helper is too painful to sustain. An undetected injury or ailment may be holding the dog back.

Slipping off the sleeve may be a combination of a weak dog and incorrect training for this specific dog. If this is the case, the problem may seem to be solved, but it will generally show up again in some form. Sometimes it will show up in growling while the helper drives the dog, or slipping from the center to the end of the sleeve because the dog cannot handle the pressure. This may be because the helper is pressuring the dog too much, or simply because the dog is emotionally weak or does not have good enough nerves for the work.

IMPROVING THE GRIP

To some degree the way a dog bites is genetic. Some dogs are born with the desire to get the bite as deep into their mouths as possible. Others bite with only the front of the mouth in the area of the canine teeth. In both cases, the bite can be either improved or ruined by the type of training the dog receives. The type of sleeve the helper is using during the different stages of training will be important because this may help or hurt the dog's grip.

When teaching and improving the grip, the dog should be on a long line attached to a post. We prefer to use a harness rather than a leather

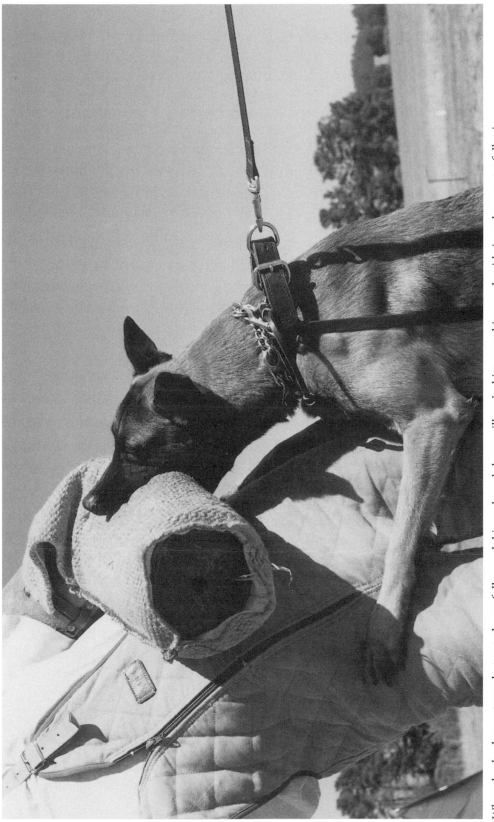

When the dog has a strong but not always full-mouth bite, a barrel sleeve will make him open his mouth wide in order to get a full grip.

collar because it does not put pressure on the dog's neck. When the helper presents the sleeve, they should stand sideways and lean away so as not to show body language that overpowers the dog. The pull should be from the shoulder with the rest of the arm relaxed. The muscles of the arm should not be tight. As the dog shows more desire for the sleeve and is committed to the bites, he should be rewarded by giving him the sleeve.

A common mistake helpers make is "rewarding" the dog with a vigorous fight when he bites well with a full mouth. This is the exact opposite of what the dog needs. The dog needs to *win* and understand that a good grip will weaken the helper. This is the only way to empower the dog.

Another way to improve the grip is to use a bungee line. This helps build more commitment because the line will pull the dog back if he attacks halfheartedly. The bungee should always be used carefully so the dog does not flip over backward and hurt himself. Again, we suggest you use a harness so the dog does not feel undue pressure on his neck.

When the dog has a full-mouth grip on the sleeve, the helper lets the dog dominate him.

Working on the grip by using a bungee line. (Debbie Dilley)

Pull the dog back far enough that there is no pressure at all on the line. The dog should be able to move forward three to four steps before feeling any pressure from the bungee. The pressure should then increase gradually, so it is at its greatest point when the dog reaches out to grip the sleeve. The handler can hold onto the line so that if the helper makes the dog miss a few times to build the desire, the dog will not go flying backward.

When the dog does grip the sleeve, the tension on the bungee line should make him hang on tighter. If he slips the bite, the fact that the release will make him go sliding backward should cause enough discomfort that he won't want to allow the same thing to happen again. The next time he gets the opportunity to grasp the sleeve, he will do so with a fuller and more solid bite.

Another technique the handler can use is the left-right miss. Presenting the sleeve to the left and right in front of the dog helps to build anticipation. This should be done just out of reach, but very close.

The dog will be lunging toward the sleeve. If he makes noise when he lunges, he is not ready to bite. He is not committed. When he stops lunging and coils, preparing to strike, let him bite. After the bite, the helper should very quickly give just a second of tension on the sleeve and then release it to the dog. This is done to show the dog that biting is not the end of the game. He may have to work harder after he bites, and therefore needs to bite harder and deeper to be successful.

BODY SUIT WORK

In most cases dogs that do not have a full grip or are showing signs of nervousness while on the sleeve suffer from a lack of confidence. We use

Warren Jones and Ivan are working on the dog's grip by making him miss several times. (Debbie Dilley)

Using a leg sleeve takes the pressure off the helper, plus the dog feels more secure with all four feet on the ground.

a full body suit from time to time with all the dogs we train. This builds their confidence and makes them pay close attention to the helper's movements (which improves targeting), doesn't enable them to be lazy during protection work and builds the fighting drive.

We find that this type of work does not confuse the dogs. They have no problems whatsoever switching back and forth from sleeve to suit work. Of course, it's important that the helper knows how to work a dog in a suit if he is to bring out the best in the dog!

When trying to improve the grip, keep in mind that the fight between the dog and the helper is always more on a psychological than a physical level. The helper should always watch for signs of stress and never overpower the dog.

Presentation of the Sleeve

The presentation of the sleeve is an important factor in Schutzhund trials. A bad sleeve presentation will result in a bad grip and a loss of points.

While in training, the sleeve should always be presented correctly for the dog to bite. Many times in an effort to make a dog's bite fuller and deeper in the mouth, the helper will try to shove the sleeve at the dog as he bites. This may seem to help at first, but you will find that since the dog himself is not choosing to do this, he will not learn anything. When the sleeve is presented correctly, he will quickly go back to a frontal bite.

A much more effective technique than stuffing him with the sleeve each time is to make the dog work harder for the bite. This does not mean putting him on the defensive. Rather, it is best to show him that the helper is not easy prey and that the dog has to work hard to catch the helper. Through this type of training, the dog gains confidence and learns a lot about the helper's overall body language and movements. He also learns how to be successful when presented with difficult situations. He can then learn to dominate the fight no matter how the helper tries to oppose him.

Here is an example of this technique. Start by working the dog on a back-tie. When the handler gives the bite command to the dog, the helper presents the sleeve. But instead of presenting it in the usual horizontal position, the helper presents it almost vertically. If the dog has not seen this before, he will most likely try to bite without turning his head sideways. This will result in a bad grip.

Some dogs will instinctively turn their heads the first time—others will not. This doesn't really say anything good or bad about the dog. The helper should not let the dog bite unless the helper sees the dog making an effort to turn his head. After the dog always turns his head when attempting to bite, it is time for the next step.

Begin the next step with the dog sitting still on the line. The helper walks within the radius of the back-tie. With the dog still sitting (so that he can focus on what is happening), the helper stands with the sleeve in any position (vertical, horizontal, high, low or by either side). The handler then sends the dog.

The helper will not move to help the dog get a good entry. The dog will have to make the entry himself and, if correct, the helper will reward him with a fight or immediately slip the sleeve. When the dog doesn't enter with a full grip, the handler should out him and try again.

The helper may decide to use an easier version of the first presentation. When the dog is able to enter correctly with different presentations from a static position, you are ready to move to more challenging exercises.

By angling the sleeve almost vertically, the dog must turn his head in order to get a full-mouth grip.

The dog is still on the back-tie, sitting still on the line. The helper stands within reach, holding the sleeve behind the back. The dog remains quietly in position. The helper will "mark" only with the sleeve, without moving other body parts. The helper does this by moving the sleeve across the body to the left or right. This enables the dog to better observe the movement and judge where he will enter. The helper will then place the sleeve back behind the body.

The handler will now give the dog a command to bite, and as the dog begins to move, the helper places the sleeve in the exact marked position. Because the dog has been exposed to this position while biting previously and the position has already been marked, the dog should be intent on the proper entry. In other words, he should already have calculated his body motion and the position from which to enter for the bite. This should so consume his thought processes that he will forget the actual grip as he enters. This can work to your benefit because many times the dog will grip better than he ever has as a result of the effort it takes to target the sleeve while it's in motion.

Ivan Balabanov and Amok Ot Vitosha, SchHIII, IPOIII. The dog will lunge right through the stick.

When the dog has mastered this challenge, it's time to add another. The sleeve will still start out behind the body, but the helper will hold the stick horizontally in front of the sleeve as if to prevent the dog from reaching his goal. This is more psychological pressure than anything else. At this stage, no portion of the stick is actually meant to oppose the dog. The dog goes right through it. You want him to be successful. The stick should end up lying against the dog's chest passively if this is done correctly.

When this step is completed successfully, you can go to the field off leash. At 20 feet from the helper, the dog can now keep an eye on the *whole* helper, not just the sleeve, and study the way the helper moves. The helper now uses two sleeves, offering one or the other at the last minute. This teaches the dog to watch the helper's body language.

It is important to present the sleeve at the right time, so that the dog will leap toward it without slowing. The helper should be able to swing the dog into the air, left, right, high and low, with the various sleeve presentations.

After an out command, sometimes the handler and helper will work on the technical aspects of the bite work. It is best, when working on technical bites, to work just on that in a single training session. This is somewhat like sparring in a boxing match, in that the dog can learn about his opponent's moves without the pressure of a serious fight.

Later, the helper can focus even more attention on his or her movements by holding one sleeve and presenting a seemingly easy bite. As the dog comes closer, the helper quickly switches to the other sleeve that is being held behind the body. Then the handler will out the dog. The helper continues to keep the dog in suspense over which sleeve will be presented on the re-bite.

If the dog is keen enough, the helper can use another technique that, if used properly, will bring out the fighting drive in a dog and make him very intense. The helper keeps the dog away from the sleeve by pushing him on his chest with the stick. This makes the dog put in an extra effort because he has to go through the stick to get the bite.

Depending on the dog, the helper decides how much pressure to use before the dog can be successful. Sticks made of various materials (such as bamboo) can be used, even though these will not be presented in a Schutzhund trial.

Teaching the Out

The out command should first be introduced to the dog while he's play-ing with a toy. You will do yourself and your dog a great favor by teaching him to let go of a toy before outing the dog off a sleeve. Your play should simulate protection work. When the dog is playing and you want him to out, freeze with the toy in your hand, just as the helper freezes, before you command your dog "out." When the dog releases the toy, he is rewarded with play again. The dog soon learns that he controls the play by complying with the command. Once he understands and complies with "out," you can transfer all the rules the dog already knows about playing with you and the toy to his bite training.

When the out off the sleeve is introduced, the dog should be worked on back-tie and should get a few "free" bites first, to somewhat satisfy his desire to bite. When the helper slips the sleeve after the first few bites, the dog can carry it around the pole and then you should command the dog to sit or lie down. Now the helper puts on another sleeve. Give the com-mand to out, and as soon as the dog releases the first sleeve, reward him with a bite. Repeat this until the dog understands that as soon as he releases the first sleeve, the helper will initiate another fight with the second sleeve.

The next step is actually outing the dog off the helper. For this part of the training, the helper should wear a sleeve on each arm. The helper gives the bite and fight as usual. But this time, when the helper stops the fight, he or she should stand still with the sleeve in front of the body and wait for the dog to release. If the dog hangs on, the helper should brace and wait. When the dog begins to release by loosening the grip, whining or changing pressure slightly, the helper should let you know—that's when you command "out." This command should not be harsh. Rather, it should seem as if you are helping the dog to make the right decision. As soon as the dog releases the sleeve, the helper should reward him with a bite on the second sleeve.

The second sleeve minimizes the natural possessiveness of the dog. Just as you would be reluctant to give up a $100 bill, the dog is reluctant to give up his sleeve. However, if you had $50 and someone asked to exchange it for an identical $50, you would be more likely to do it because you aren't losing anything. Psychologically, two sleeves are the same thing to the dog. He releases one sleeve but obtains another.

Here Ivan makes his best effort to push the dog away with the stick

—which only leads to greater determination on the dog's part!

Using two sleeves helps to reinforce the out. (Debbie Dilley)

It's very important for the helper not to move or provoke the dog in any way before the dog actually releases the sleeve. When the helper stands still, the bite is no longer reinforcing. It is then in the dog's best interest to release and wait until the helper moves again before re-biting. Also, if the helper puts too much pressure on the dog when fighting, the dog will become more reluctant to let go of his reward.

Toward the end of the session, the helper should offer a bite and then stand still without intimidating the dog. You should remain close to the dog and after a second or two, command him to out. If the dog does the out, he should be rewarded immediately with a re-bite. The helper should then slip the sleeve and you should take the dog off the field.

During the next few sessions, start by giving some free bites, but, as the session goes on, ask the dog to out more frequently. It's important in this stage to wait with the command until the helper freezes and the dog calms down a bit.

PROBLEMS WITH THE OUT

The "out" command can be touchy with dogs. Too much work with the helper on the out can be harmful to a dog that does not yet have the confidence or commitment to bite. On the other hand, avoiding outs for too long can set you up for later difficulties with this command.

Relying solely on physical corrections for a dog with problems can create conflict between the dog and the helper, the dog and you, or all three. There is a natural conflict in the dog when he is engaged in a fight and someone tries to pull him out of it. He will tend to resist the pressure and even bite and hold on harder.

When the dog has problems with the out command, you and the helper should be able to figure out whether the problem is due to a strong desire and drive to bite, or is the result of insecurity or a lack of control. You cannot solve the problem properly unless you know this.

The dog that is determined to bite and has difficulty on the out may shake the sleeve himself when the helper freezes. This dog should be worked on a tie-out to hold him in place. When the dog is at the end of the line and it is stretched to the limit, he will not have the flexibility to keep up the fight, as he would if he had no restrictions. When he is told to out at the end of the line, the helper can reach around and hold the sleeve still with a free hand. The helper should refuse to let the sleeve move at all. Because of the tie-out line (and because you are holding him), the dog should not be able to move either, and will soon tire of standing on his hind legs with the sleeve in his mouth. To take the pressure off his mouth and legs, he will have to let go. When he does, you should encourage him to sit, yet still intensely watch the helper. When the helper moves again, he can then spring into action.

As soon as the dog understands that the rules of the game are that he must let go before the fight begins again, he will comply. At this point, the game should always end with the dog getting the sleeve as a reward. This way, the dog will not fear that the bite will end with the helper walking away with the sleeve.

To teach a dog that is insecure, you must use a method that does not create a lot of conflict in the dog. You will still be using a tie-out. After the dog gives a standard bite, have the helper fight briefly with the dog, then slip the sleeve and allow the dog to run around with it. While the dog is enjoying his prize, the helper puts on another sleeve and tries to get the dog's attention on the new sleeve. You should then let the dog go for the sleeve on the helper.

Play out this same sequence again and again. When you see that the dog is willing to spit out the sleeve in less time in order to go for the one on the handler, it is time to start commanding "out" before letting him go for the second sleeve. The helper should reward the dog with the other sleeve as soon as possible after the dog releases the first sleeve.

For the dog that lacks control, either of these methods can be used. It is not unusual for the dog to prefer either the left or the right sleeve. If your dog has a preference, you can use this to your advantage in training. First use the sleeve he doesn't like as much. He will then be more willing to release it to you in favor of the preferred sleeve.

To wean the dog off two-sleeve work, do a whole series of bites and outs (three to four quick ones in a row). At the end, reward the whole series by slipping the sleeve. Following this, the dog should be able to do the whole series with only one sleeve.

The next step is to introduce stick hits. Do not command an out right after the stick hits because the dog will need time to calm down. Stick hits tend to make the dog more determined to hang on, and thus you would be working against yourself. The first few times you should wait long enough for the dog to calm down before you try the out. Gradually shorten the time you wait between stick hits and outs, until you can out the dog even after the pressure of the stick hits.

If the dog is not willing to out after the stick hits, the helper can pull him forward to the end of the tie-out and then wait for him to let go as we described earlier in the chapter. Depending on how the dog responds, the helper can then reward the dog for releasing by giving a second bite. Alternatively, if the dog is being stubborn, the helper can give the ultimate punishment by setting the sleeve down and walking away. This is like saying, "All right, if you won't play by the rules, we won't play."

If the outs are coming along nicely on the tie-out, you can start introducing bite work on the open field. You should always begin with the dog on the line and make sure everything is going well before you take the line off. If, at this point, you feel that you need to make a physical correction, you must make sure it requires only one or two jerks *toward* the sleeve; otherwise, you will be nagging the dog and this will cause more harm than good. It is important not to pull the dog to the back or side because you can dislodge his teeth.

The most common way to reinforce the out is by correcting from a long line or with a correction that comes from the helper. Both of these corrections will lead to some avoidance from the dog (toward the helper or the handler, depending on who's giving the correction).

The Ultimate Punishment

When the dog does protection work he's always in high drive, which makes it very difficult to control him. This is when some trainers will use a lot of physical corrections to teach and maintain the desired behavior. But we've found that along with correcting the unwanted behavior, physical corrections cause avoidance in the dog and affect other behaviors that we don't necessarily want to change.

While the use of electronic collars is common in protection work, we strongly advise you to use great caution with them. The risk of using one on a dog that is not suitable for an e-collar, or using one incorrectly, is great. Only seasoned professionals who know how to use them correctly should make the determination of how and when to use the e-collar.

In any case, physical corrections aren't as effective as reward withholding techniques, and they must be used more often. As we said when we described our training methods in Chapter 4, we like to simply withhold the reward as punishment whenever possible. Then the dog isn't relying on the handler's help (even if the help is a correction)—he has to actually think and find out for himself what works and what doesn't. This is ultimately a better way to reinforce the proper behavior.

Obviously, during protection training the best reward for the dog is the fight and the sleeve. To show the dog that he did something wrong, we withhold the highly desired reward—the sleeve. We spend a great deal of time conditioning the dog to know that when the helper drops the sleeve or puts it on the ground, the action has stopped and there will be no fight. The dog eventually understands that once the sleeve is down he should not go and grab it, but instead should try a different behavior to initiate the fight. We call this technique *the ultimate punishment* because it is the worst possible punishment for a dog doing bite work. Once the dog understands how to respond, this technique can be applied in *all* correction situations in bite work.

USING THE ULTIMATE PUNISHMENT TECHNIQUE

Teaching the dog to respond to the ultimate punishment has to be done in a very controlled environment. The dog must be on a harness with a long line tied to a post. He should already have a good understanding of basic obedience commands because now is not the time to teach them. Remember, you'll try to help the dog figure out what is correct, but it will take a while for him to actually ask for help—he'll be too busy barking, lunging and trying everything he can to get at the helper first.

Position the dog on a sit about five feet from the end of the long line, and stand next to him. The helper stands in a nonconfrontational way about one to two feet away from the "entry zone" (the area where the dog can reach the helper). If the dog wants to break his position because he sees the helper, do not restrain him—let him try. The long line will not allow him close enough to bite the helper.

If the dog breaks the sit, the helper will drop the sleeve, but not right in front of the dog; the helper will drop it four to five feet from the dog and walk away. What's happening here is the dog was asked to sit but chose to break the command in order to get to the action—except now he can't reach it.

The helper continues to stay away in a nonengaging manner, and the sleeve is just lying on the ground. While the dog is lunging back and forth, barking and pulling trying to get to the sleeve, you should leave him alone—the dog is in such high drive that any command will not be obeyed. In any case, the dog doesn't yet need your help to solve this puzzle. You should just be holding the long line high, so the dog doesn't get tangled or injured.

Depending on the dog, it may take a while for him to give up and stop lunging. When the dog doesn't give up, you need to be patient and just wait. This tenacity is actually a desirable trait in a Schutzhund dog, and you don't want to discourage it. He is showing his desire for the fight. Sooner or later there will be a moment when a big question mark "appears" above the dog's head. "What's going on?" he asks himself. This is when you should step in and ask him once again to sit or heel by your side. This should not be a forceful command, but more like, "Do you want to sit now?" Remember, you're trying to help, not force the dog to do something he doesn't want to do.

Typically, the moment the dog hears your voice he will start trying again to get to the helper without even thinking about what you just said. Let him try again and work even harder. Once again he will quit in disgust and confusion. If he makes brief eye contact or just stays there wondering what to do, it's time once again to try to help him by calmly giving another sit or heel command.

It doesn't really matter which command you give, as long as you are not giving four or five different commands. The goal here is to show the dog that the only way to get to the action is by listening to you and obeying what you say. That's why you should choose commands that your dog performs very well outside of protection training.

Eventually the dog will obey your obedience commands. As soon as he does, the helper picks up the sleeve and you give the bite command. If the dog enjoys the fight, the helper should hold onto the sleeve for a few moments but without putting any more fuel on the fire. The dog is already highly frustrated and eager. Then the helper should slip the sleeve to the dog and walk away.

The dog can hold onto the sleeve for a while if he wants to. Whether he holds or drops it, you should place the dog on a sit or down and bring the sleeve back to the helper. As soon as you go to pick up the sleeve, the dog is very likely to break the command, get up and go into high drive again. If that happens, drop the sleeve right where it was, step sideways a few feet away from the dog and wait until he decides to stop lunging. Then ask the dog to sit or down again. If he obeys, go and pick up the sleeve. Do this over and over again until the dog stops breaking his sit or down.

You must not become frustrated about it or forceful with your commands. Once you are able to get the sleeve, hand it to the helper and return to the dog, he may again decide it is time to start the action. The helper will put the sleeve down, and you should again walk away. When the dog is calm, ask him to sit or down again. If he complies, reward him with the command to attack as the helper picks up the sleeve and gives a bite right away without any additional excitement.

You want to work toward a progression in which the dog obeys the command, you walk to the helper with the sleeve, you return to your dog, you ask for another obedience command, the dog obeys the command and is given a bite as his reward.

The first few sessions will be highly frustrating for the dog (and for you!), but then you will start to see changes in the dog's behavior. When the sleeve goes down, the dog will start looking to you for help, or perhaps will offer one of the obedience commands even without being asked. This is a sign that he is starting to understand that the sleeve being down is a form of punishment. More important, he understands how to respond to it: by "asking" for another try. Now you can start to work on teaching the exact rules of the exercise. Soon the dog will go back to you and wait willingly for a command when the sleeve reward is withheld.

This ultimate punishment sequence is used for all control exercises: blind searches, hold and bark, transports, bumping and pushing the helper or the sleeve, and breaking the down and sit commands. For example, when the dog skips a blind and goes straight to the helper, the sleeve goes down and the dog automatically returns to his handler ready for another try.

The Dog that Misses Blinds

There is more than one way to teach the dog to go around the blinds. One is to keep the dog in the dark, not knowing where the helper is. To do this, the dog is walked off the field after the helper hides in the first blind. The helper then moves to another blind. When the dog goes to the original hiding place, he is surprised to find nothing there and is directed to the next blind, where he does find the helper and is rewarded.

This technique works, but it may actually prolong the learning process and can create problems down the road. All the dog knows is that we are saying "go find him." If the dog knows where the bad guy is hiding on the day of the trial, he may feel that he doesn't need to run the blinds. From the dog's point of view, it's a waste of time to search when he already knows where the bad guy is.

Instead of trying to fool the dog, we prefer the direct approach. This approach teaches the dog to go around the blinds because this is *the only way to initiate the fight.* This is important psychologically because it has everything to do with the dog being reliable.

The training begins by placing a food or toy reward inside the blind. We prefer the toy, but the principle is the same with either one. You can even do this exercise as a game when the dog is as young as five to eight months of age, but you should have a reliable sit and down command established before teaching the blinds.

To start as a game, have a tug toy attached to the end of a long line. Place the toy next to the outside edge of the blind, with the line running behind the blind to the opposite side. Stand at your dog's side with the end of the line in your hand. Send the dog with the command ("reviere," "voran," "search" or whatever you use), and use the hand signal to direct him toward the blind. As your dog goes toward the toy, pull the line so that the toy disappears behind the blind. (You will have to change your position when you pull to slightly angle toward the right; otherwise the toy will get caught in the blind.) Continue to pull on it so that the dog has to go around the blind and come back toward you before he gets the toy. Play with the dog and the toy for a short time, and then repeat the process.

Once your dog is playing this game without running back the way he came or having any difficulties, you are ready for the next step. Place the toy in the blind or far enough around the other side that he can no longer see it. Show him the toy as you enter the blind and smack it on the ground with a loud enough sound that he knows it is there, even though it's not visible. Go back to the dog and then run the same exercise we just described. You should now be close to the blind when he finds the toy. Play with him again.

The next step is to do this again, except you will smack the toy on the ground but then keep it hidden on your person. When you send the dog this time, you will meet him on the other side of the blind with the toy in your hand and offer to play with it. When he does this willingly, the last step in this series is for you to do the entire exercise, making sure the dog comes around the blind and calling him to you, offering the toy. Now he has completed the search of one blind in order to get what he wants from you, the toy.

You should now be able to leave the toy in your pocket and send the dog around the blind. (You will periodically have to leave the toy in the blind so that the dog will never be sure what you will do.) If the dog is confused at first, be patient. You can take a few steps toward the blind while giving the hand signal. As soon as the dog goes around the blind, be sure to show the toy and play.

At about this point in the training, the dog will likely try to steal the toy or get you to play without running the blind. It is important to be firm and make him understand that he will not get to play unless he runs the blind. Once you have this understanding, the rest of the training and the dog's reliability from then on will be easily established. It is important to strike a balance with your firmness and not to overcorrect, or you will risk backsliding on your training.

The next step in training the blinds is to start moving from blind to blind. Make the dog complete each blind individually—not in rapid succession, but one at a time, always with a reward offered at the end of each success. When this is accomplished, the fastest way to progress further is to use portable blinds set up about 20 feet apart. Send the dog to the first one, and then call him back and reward. Sit him facing the second one and do the same, and so on. Next, increase the distance between the blinds a little at a time, until you finally have them at the normal trial distance.

Now you want to stagger the times when you will offer a reward. Sometimes you'll reward after one blind, sometimes after three or maybe only after all six. You want to stagger the rewards to keep the dog from generalizing when the reward will be given.

After the dog can run all six blinds, it's time to introduce the helper onto the field. The helper now takes the place of the reward. The dog gets to bite when he runs the blinds.

We start by using two blinds a short distance apart. The dog knows where the helper is at this point. Position the dog closer to the blind that he has to go around first—the one without the helper. If the dog goes straight to the blind with the helper, he must learn that if he tries to cheat and refuses to run the blinds, the helper will not play. Instead, the helper will put the sleeve down and walk off the field. This is not what the dog wants. Soon he will learn that by running the blinds he will get what he wants. From this point, the helper can be put in various positions, both in and out of the blinds, in order to reward the dog for going around them.

Martha Hoffman's Amok Ot Vitosha working the blinds.

We will explain more about how the helper can help you gain control of the dog later in this chapter in the section "Power Struggles on the Field."

Problems with the Bark and Hold

During the bark and hold exercise, the dog has to show a high level of confidence. Ideally, his bark will be strong and consistent while guarding the helper. The dog should be intense and ready to bite at any time if the helper attempts to escape.

If you see a dog being defensive during this exercise, tail tucked, ears back or keeping a distance from the helper, it may be because of the way the exercise was taught. This generally happens when too much compulsion has been applied in order to keep the dog "clean" (no inappropriate bites). Other dogs may bark almost playfully, as if begging the helper to move so they can bite. Such a dog is focused more on the sleeve than the helper, and generally yips in a higher tone. He is more relaxed than he should be. The true desired response is intensity.

With most dogs we start teaching the bark and hold using the helper right away. This creates the proper barking response from the start.

The way the helper works the dog will depend largely on which drive the dog is working in. If the helper puts more pressure on the dog than he can handle, the dog will display avoidance behavior: ears back, hackles up, leaning backward, showing a lot of teeth and gums while barking, and so on. You do not want this! Instead, you are looking for intensity and confidence in his performance.

The bark and hold is the exercise where the helper likes to use a lot of tools, such as the stick and the whip. In Schutzhund, the stick and whip are used to make noise and to imitate weapons that may hurt a dog. The helper's tools, however, are padded and made so they will not hurt the dog.

How the helper uses the whip or stick will directly affect the dog's response. If the helper cracks the whip repeatedly and moves quickly, he will incite the dog's prey drive. If the helper's body language is such that he overwhelms the dog, corners him with the stick or hits him with the stick, he will be eliciting the dog's defense drive.

The dog should not have to rely on the helper's movements to stimulate him for long. You want the dog to be able to respond on his own to a helper standing still. When the dog comes into the blind where the helper is standing still, the line the dog is training on should be held in such a position by the handler (or an assistant) that the dog cannot get quite close enough to be able to bite the helper. The helper should then excite the dog only as necessary.

The dog should not be allowed to obtain the sleeve as the reward unless he barks first. At first, one or two barks will do. As the dog realizes that the barking pleases you and results in gratification, withhold the sleeve until he barks more.

Some dogs' first instinct when they're excited is to bark. This is the easiest type of dog to train for a bark and hold. Other dogs will stalk up to the blind in a crouch and stare at the helper in a hunting mode. This type of dog is harder to teach to bark. You can try many different scenarios, such as having the dog on a tie-out, behind a fence, in a car or in a doorway, to see what gets him barking.

In some cases, the bark command has to be taught separately at home. This might be done by getting the dog excited over food or a toy. It may take longer to get a dog of this nature to bark if he is an older dog.

But it is important that once the dog does bark, the command is reinforced both verbally and with a reward.

At first, the helper may reward even the smallest whine with the sleeve in order to get the dog to understand that vocalization is what you desire. Once the dog catches on and begins to vocalize more readily, you can be more discriminating about when to reward the dog.

The distance between the dog and the helper will affect the type of bark the dog uses. The helper should seek to recognize a dog's comfort zone and work within it. As the training progresses, the comfort zone should shrink, allowing the helper to be closer to the dog. If the dog is not comfortable and moves away, the helper needs to adjust his body position to a side profile or a stance that makes him appear weaker. If the opposite is true and the dog's barking is high-pitched and excited, the helper should move slowly toward the dog only when he barks in a deeper pitch. The dog will soon associate the deeper barks with being able to bring the helper to him.

The bark and hold is often worked in the beginning of a training session while the dog is fresh and easily provoked into high drive. Although some dogs will need the helper to give them two or three bites before they are fully engaged in drive, other dogs may be best stimulated to bark through sheer frustration.

The first technique we use to build frustration is to back-tie the dog to a post. You should put him in a sit position with the helper out of sight. As the helper enters the field, the dog should not be allowed to bark. On the back-tie, the dog should be told to bite. The helper will present the bite, but then pull it away at the last second. He will make the dog miss repeatedly, giving several quick left-right presentations of the sleeve. The dog should be so preoccupied with the desire to bite that he doesn't make any noise. The helper then stands still in front of the dog, which will frustrate him and give him the opportunity to bark. The helper stands still until the dog unloads his stress by barking. He then gives the dog a bite.

A harness should be used with this technique to alleviate pressure on the dog's neck. You should also take care not to let the dog make leaps that take him off his feet. The dog could injure himself if you do not take hold of the tie-out and keep him down low enough that he cannot launch himself into the air.

Yet another technique to build frustration and get the dog to bark is to hide the helper in a blind. The idea is to make the dog think he can make the helper appear by barking. The dog should be on a line held by you 10 feet from the blind. The helper steps out of the blind, excites the dog, and then jumps back in. When the dog barks, the helper jumps out and allows the dog to bite. This sequence is repeated several times until the dog understands that he must bark several times in order to get the bite reward.

The final way we will mention is to have you and the dog on one side of a chain-link fence panel and the helper on the other. A 10- to 12-foot-long chain-link panel usually works well for this. The helper agitates the dog, frustrating him because the helper is on the other side of the fence. When the dog is finally frustrated enough to bark, the helper runs to the end of the fence and allows the dog to bite.

Staying Clean in the Blind

Teaching the dog to stay clean in the blind and not bite inappropriately is the next step after teaching the dog to bark. The dog is now asked to go into the blind and stand off the bad guy without biting, pushing, nipping or otherwise harassing him.

At this point, the dog is barking fairly close to the helper and realizes that barking brings a reward. The next step is to have the helper close enough that if the dog wanted to bite, he could. The helper will now slowly push in toward the dog. At the same time, the arm with the sleeve remains still.

As the dog backs up and barks, he will ultimately be rewarded with the sleeve. If, on the other hand, the dog barks and then bites, you will correct the dog using the line and the action ceases. Then start the exercise all over again, until the dog understands that the right thing to do is continue to bark until the helper escalates the action by attempting to become aggressive or escape.

This is another place where we use the ultimate punishment to correct undesired behaviors. To punish the action of the dog that wishes to bite on the bark and hold, the helper simply drops the sleeve on the ground and walks away.

Here is an example. The handler puts the dog on a long line and sends him to do a bark and hold. The dog barrels toward the helper with the intent of biting. The dog is brought up short on the leash so he does not get the reward that he seeks. The helper then backs up a couple of steps and puts the sleeve on the ground and walks away.

A correct guarding position without bothering the helper.

The next seven photos show the ultimate punishment sequence. Start with your dog on a sit next to you.

The dog bumps or nips at the sleeve while the helper stands still.

The helper refuses to engage in a fight by dropping the sleeve out of the dog's reach.

With the sleeve on the ground, the dog will eventually figure out that he must follow commands, or else there will be no fight.

When the sleeve is withheld, the dog learns that he must return to you.

The handler asks the dog to sit.

The dog complies, and the sequence begins again.

The dog will soon realize that if the game is not played as the helper wishes it to be played, the game is over. The process is repeated until the dog is not quite sure what is being asked of him. He will go toward the helper, but without the previous vigor and stop short of the line. At this point, the sleeve is given. The dog realizes that the effective response was to stop short of the decoy. The final picture should be a dog that runs down the field, puts on the brakes in front of the helper and displays an intense, deep bark.

The next step is to put the helper in the blind and condition the dog that this is where the hold and bark is done. The helper can do some left and right misses in order to frustrate the dog, and then run into the blind. You should then proof the dog even further by going into a field, having the helper run and, as the dog is sent, turn around and freeze. The dog should go to a bark and hold. If he does not, the sleeve is dropped as a correction and the exercise is started again.

The dog must also learn the opposite exercise: Even though he is sent on a bark and hold, if the helper immediately fights or flees, the dog has to initiate an apprehension. This allows the dog to think and gives him the freedom to understand that if the helper runs, the dog can change the mode he is in.

CREATING THE RIGHT ATTITUDE

As we mentioned in the description of the hold and bark exercise in Chapter 9, the rule book says the dog must show persistence; it must be self-assured, attentive and intense. To create this attitude in a dog, trainers use compulsion to build and to control drive. But as we explained in Chapter 4, a dog will react one of four ways to compulsion: aggression, fleeing, submitting or freezing.

When using compulsion in this situation, the trainer tries to put just enough pressure on the dog to provoke an aggressive reaction, but not so much that the dog becomes overly defensive. This aggressive reaction is created by the frustration caused by the compulsion (an avoidance response), the agitation and the control commands. Many dogs who are trained in such a way will also show undesirable effects of the avoidance response, such as nervousness, fear and defensiveness.

When using the ultimate punishment we create only frustration, which brings the dog into the desired attitude. We do not create the avoidance that would arise from a physical correction. This helps control the drive.

Because the dog is under control, when released he starts right away with the desired attitude, avoiding the few seconds of settling that are so typical of the dogs trained through physical compulsion.

Power Struggles on the Field

There is nothing more rewarding for a good Schutzhund dog than fighting with the helper and winning the sleeve! Because of this, the most difficult thing for the dog to learn is *not to fight with the helper* to get the sleeve. This is the type of power struggle that exists in various aspects of the training, but none more than the bark and hold exercise. The dog will always want to test to see if he can take a cheap shot in the blind, skip a blind when searching for the helper or forge at him during the transport. All of these exercises have one common denominator: They require control from the dog, whose desire is to gain satisfaction through engaging the helper.

A large portion of our training consists of working on these control issues. The most traditional ways to keep control of the dog rely on compulsion. Trainers make the dog obey by using a series of physical corrections. These corrections include things like long lines with pinch collars (not allowed at trials), short tabs for helpers to grab and correct, electric collars, electric sleeves, barricades in front of the helper, or three or four assistant trainers to help correct on the field. All of these techniques may help from time to time. However, you run a real risk that the dog will soon realize none of these corrections are ever used in a trial. The trial-wise dog will make control mistakes at the trial and will lose points.

We prefer to take a different approach. It takes a little longer to effect a change in the dog's behavior, but the change lasts a lot longer. The traditional forms of physical correction tend to make the dog overly aware of the handler and perhaps a bit sensitive because he is anticipating a correction. Our more psychological approach will eliminate the conflict in the dog.

Since the dog wants to get to the helper with the sleeve, this is exactly what you should let him do. Take a toy to the field and play with the dog. Have the helper appear on the field with the sleeve. When the dog sees him, he will want to run over and engage him in a fight. As he does, the helper should just set the sleeve down and walk away.

Testing Control

The final test, to see if the dog understands that he is not to be obsessed with the idea of engaging the helper, is to:

1. Send him, allow a bite and a fight, and give the dog the sleeve.
2. Give the sleeve back to the helper, who should set up as he would to engage the dog.
3. Call the dog to play with the toy. He should accept the toy or sleeve equally.

When this is working, you can do the same test with the blinds. Call the dog to you when he's running the blinds and sometimes reward him with a toy. This means the dog understands that when you call him to you, you actually mean *to you*, not past you and into the next blind.

At the same time, you should make a big production about having the toy and call the dog back. If the dog seems confused and wants to stay near the sleeve and helper (just in case he may get a bite), stay calm. Calmly invite the dog to play. Eventually, the dog will tire of waiting and will return to you. Give him a good game.

After a few lessons using this style of correction, the dog will learn that he does not control when he can engage the helper. He learns that there are *rules of engagement*. Once the dog understands that you and the helper control the reward, he will calm down and the conflict within him will subside. It may take some time to effect this change in the dog, but it will be worth the wait if you want to have 100 percent control of your dog on the field.

When you follow this philosophy, the work will become easier and you'll progress faster as a result of the dog's clear head and confidence. *This is because you will have effectively eliminated the conflict that is the product of a power struggle.*

Competition at the National and World Levels

When you're competing at the advanced levels of Schutzhund, it's likely your goal will be to attend the national and international trials. These trials, with all their traveling and unfamiliar surroundings, can be tough on your dog and on you.

As veterans of many competitions, we'd like to share some tips about how to make your travel smoother and get the most out of your dog.

Getting Ready for the Trial

Everyone wants to get the best results for the time they spend training before a Schutzhund trial. One of the most common mistakes people make is that in their enthusiasm, they overwork the dog. More is not always better!

To get good results, Schutzhund training should be done three times a week. Cover all three phases every week, but not necessarily in each training session. Depending on the dog's age and energy level, you may end up doing one more or less practice session to suit your dog. A well-trained, seasoned Schutzhund dog that doesn't have any particular problems to work out may be maintained with a session once a week or even less. The intensity in any given handler's training will also vary, depending on the problems that need to be worked out before a trial.

One of the main things you want to avoid is burning the dog out. This can happen when you work so hard before the trial that the dog gives his peak performance in training. His work may then go downhill on the day of the trial.

When problems need to be worked out before a trial, you should allow enough time to solve the problems, get rid of avoidance behaviors and have four to five successful sessions before the competition takes place. You should not be fixing problems a week before the trial. This is also not the time to be trying out new training techniques.

With that said, it can still be tempting to try to work out a problem just before a trial. When you're trying to figure out if the risk is worth the possible gain, calculate how many points you're likely to lose if you leave the problem alone, and how many you may gain if you try to work out the problem. Obviously, points are important in Schutzhund. It is, after all, a competition where the participants are trying to earn the highest possible score. You will have a certain expectation of the score your dog is capable of, and how many points he may lose for his individual weaknesses. Every dog has a strong phase in the sport. For some, it may be tracking; for others, obedience or protection. But it is the *total* score that is important. Instead of making up two or three points in the phase that is the weakest for your dog, you may be able to make up those points in a phase of training that your dog does very well on. However, if you burn him out with too much training before the trial, that won't be possible.

In fact, training should *decrease* just before the trial. Just as with human athletes, it is best not to work the dog the day before a trial. He should also have total rest for three hours before the trial because forced relaxation will facilitate the best performance. The idea is to let all of his drive and energy build up.

If the dog isn't ready in terms of his training by the day before the trial, you should be realistic about your expected results or think about pulling out of the competition. Cramming in training at the last minute will create stress and bring down the dog's performance.

Traveling with a Dog

It is very important to condition your dog to travel before you take him to a trial away from home. Your dog should be conditioned to car and air travel, to travel with others and to being left in a crate in unfamiliar places such as hotel rooms. If you don't get him used to traveling ahead of time, you may regret it on the day of the trial.

A good way to have your dog practice traveling is to go to other states, visiting Schutzhund clubs. This way the dog gets used to travel, various locations and all kinds of Schutzhund fields at the same time.

Make sure you take the dog's regular food as well as bottled water. You don't want him to end up with an upset stomach from a change in diet or water. This means taking your own treats and tracking bait, too. You may also want to take some Pedialyte in case it is exceptionally hot or your dog is dehydrated from diarrhea.

Keeping the dog cool can be challenging in some climates. A raised wooden floor in the bottom of your crate allows for extra airflow and can keep the dog cooler. Also, "cool packs," originally developed to keep fire fighters cool, are available in crate sizes and can work for your dog, as long as he will not chew them up.

In preparation for a change of climate (either warmer or colder), you may wish to acclimatize the dog before you go. You can do this simply by turning up the heat or the air-conditioning where the dog spends the majority of his time. When traveling to a place that is very different in climate or elevation, you should always plan to arrive at least three days before the trial to allow your dog time to adjust.

When traveling to tracking fields, dogs are usually loaded in the luggage compartment of a bus, or in a van with other dogs. This is especially true in foreign countries. The handlers may be transported separately from the dogs. If this is your dog's first time being transported under such conditions, he may be nervous. That's why it's a good idea from time to time to have your dog ride with another trainer and their dogs to and from the practice field.

Keep in mind that you and your dog may both be required to walk a mile or so to the tracking field. You can simulate this as well in your practice sessions.

Security Considerations

Wherever you may be, it is important to know where your dog is at all times. This goes for practice trials, when you're watching the competition and everywhere else. Unfortunately, there are people who go around stealing dogs at the big events. These people know that some of the best dogs in the world are competing, and if they can steal one, they will. Even if you know your vehicle is locked and you know your dog won't let anyone come close, think again! These people know what they are doing, and will do whatever is necessary to get your dog.

You also have to guard your passport, money and credit cards. Don't take anything for granted. There are dog buyers at these events carrying a lot of money. Again, people know this and you could be a target. Remember that your mere presence in another country is a signal to some people that you have money. After all, you could afford to get there!

For a very small investment, simple devices like window locks, portable alarms and motion detectors can go a long way in helping with your security. It is also a good idea to look into the crime rates in the area where you will be traveling, as well as any particularly crime-ridden neighborhoods because every large city has good and bad sections.

Traveling Abroad

Make sure you brief yourself on the local laws and customs before entering any country. Remember that when you are in another country, you and your dog are subject to its laws and customs. It's important to know what can and cannot be legally brought into a country. And you will go a long way toward representing your country well if you attempt to conform to the customs of the place where you are. Many a guest in a foreign country has taken the stance that the country will just have to adjust to them. This is not only impolite and arrogant, it is asking for trouble. Americans have a reputation for this overseas. Since we represent our country when we travel for the U.S. Team (or your particular country's

Travel Information from Uncle Sam

The U.S. State Department offers a wide array of travel tips, brochures and advisories. You can find out what's going on currently by checking out their Web site at http://travel.state.gov or by writing to Public Information, Bureau of Public Affairs, Room 6808, U.S. Department of State, Washington, DC 20520-6810, or calling (202) 647-6575.

Schutzhund is truly an international sport.

team), we should attempt to be as polite as possible when we are guests in someone else's land.

To find out about the laws and customs in another country, you can check out books and travel guides in local libraries and consulates. The U.S. government also offers free advice to travelers and periodic reports on security issues.

Traveling by Air

When traveling with your dog by airplane, the rule is to *always check and double-check.* Call the airline far in advance of your trip, and listen carefully to all the instructions you receive. Next, verify this information with a second person at the airline, making sure everything matches up. People make mistakes sometimes when giving you flight times or transfer times. Unfortunately, these mistakes can greatly affect you and your dog, so make sure to double-check. Also, things can change the morning of the flight, so again, last-minute calls to check on flight times are wise.

The most important thing you can do is *make sure the dog gets on the airplane with you!* We cannot tell you how many people have arrived at their destinations, only to find out that their dogs were not on the plane.

In one instance, a French team of dog and handler were flying from Southern California to a seminar in Chicago, and then to Michigan. The first leg of the flight departed from Southern California and connected with another flight in Dallas, Texas. In Dallas, the dog was put on the wrong flight. The handler arrived in Chicago without a dog. After three hours of panic, the dog was located but could not arrive until the next morning.

Three days later they were to leave Chicago for a short flight to Michigan. A well-intentioned airline baggage handler tried to give the dog water. The dog broke loose and was running around on the tarmac as the unsuspecting owner was on the flight, taking off. The dog, a French Ring III title holder, eventually escaped from the airport and spent a week loose in Chicago. Only through the persistence of the sponsoring U.S. clubs, which generated television news coverage, was the dog located a week later and reunited with the handler!

This is your worst-case scenario. This is the nightmare you want to prevent. There are a few things you can do to help ensure this will not happen to you.

1. Check the airline's reputation for carrying animals before choosing that airline as your carrier. Some airlines definitely have better reputations than others. We cannot mention names here, but they are generally known among dog people, so ask around.

2. Some airlines will notify you at your seat that your dog has been safely loaded on the plane. Ask if this is possible.

3. Make sure you get your dog to the airport at least an hour before the flight, so there is time to load him (check with your airline because they may require even more time).

4. Most people do not want their dog's crate opened for any reason. You should write this on the crate. Unfortunately, as was the case with the Ring III dog, the attendant opened it anyway. To prevent this from happening, some handlers use plastic ties that hold the crate closed. They have to be cut off in order to open the crate. Others will thread the ends of the metal doors and screw in

bolts, making it impossible to open the door without a pair of pliers. This is a good idea, since some dogs learn to arch their backs and pop open a crate door by themselves.

5. Put something visual, such as a fluorescent orange strip of tape, on the top of your crate. This way, if you are traveling with several people who have crates, you can easily spot yours from the window of an airplane.

6. Be the "squeaky wheel" about your dog. If the flight attendant is racing around, asking you to sit down and assuring you that your dog will be put on, tell the attendant that you will not sit down and relax until he or she can confirm that your dog is on board. Watch out the window for the baggage cart. You should see your crate. It may be on a separate cart.

7. Most mix-ups occur when catching connecting flights. If you have time between flights, collect your dog and give him water and a bathroom break. This will enable you to make sure that he's calm and comfortable, and that he makes it to the next leg of the journey. If your flights are close together, check with the airline ahead of time to ensure that the dog will be transported directly. On international flights, this may not be possible, due to Customs. Airports treat dogs like baggage, so remember to check where your dog will be located between flights. Again, with connecting flights, be the squeaky wheel. Make the flight attendants check to see that your dog is on board before you take off.

8. Do not feed your dog for 24 hours before travel time. This way, he will not be uncomfortable because he needs to relieve himself. Make sure he drinks water before he flies (because he may have a long trip in warm conditions), but not too much.

Potty Breaks

Don't take it for granted that your dog will naturally relieve himself when given the chance. Many times, under the stress of travel dogs will become constipated and will refuse to go when you want them to. If you are at a hotel, your options of where you can take your dog to relieve himself may be limited.

It can become frustrating to take your dog in and out of your room waiting for him to go. Your best bet is to teach your dog to relieve himself on command—first at home on a leash, then locally away from home and finally out of town on practice trips. Your dog can learn this easily if it's not taught under stressful conditions.

Some people use specific scents to condition the dog to go when he smells that smell. There are scented drops for this. Others condition their dogs from the time they are pups to go in cedar shavings. When they travel, they just bring enough shavings along (in a zipper close bag, for instance), and the dog will go where the chips are placed.

A good handler should always bring along a waste control system, so you never leave dog droppings anywhere you go.

First Aid

Be self-sufficient when it comes to first aid for you and your dog. You should bring along the basics of an emergency first aid kit: bandages, scissors, bloat tube and painkillers (for you and the dog). Be prepared for bee stings, snake bites, punctures, cuts and scrapes.

Know the location of the veterinarian nearest to your hotel and to the Schutzhund field, and what you can expect of the services available to you. There is nothing worse than trying to figure these things out in an emergency.

Good Sportsmanship

Schutzhund is a sport that requires so much time, effort and patience from both the handler and the dog that anyone who walks onto the field at the National or World Championship level is, in a way, already a winner. It would be nice if everyone had this attitude and were pleasant to each other during a trial. While this is sometimes true, unfortunately, sometimes it is not.

As in any competition, egos can sometimes get in the way. Tempers can flair and things can be said. In the end, though, remember that the loser is the one who loses his or her cool. Win or lose, you can represent your club, your state or your country with pride.

After all is said and done, every man, woman and dog on the field is only truly competing against themselves. *You* start with 100 points in each exercise. *You* are responsible for any of the points subtracted. And if *you* have trained hard and smart, *you* will have the best chance of success. If *you* keep *your* attention on what *you* have to do, *nobody else will have any effect on you, one way or the other.* This is the formula for good sportsmanship and for success!

Some Final Thoughts

In the previous pages, we have laid out a style of training that is rooted in psychology and working in harmony with your dog's drives. Although the elements of Schutzhund can be taught using many different styles of training, it is our belief that none can do so with a more positive effect on the dog psychologically. And this positive effect ultimately will show in the dog's performance.

Regardless of the method you use in training your Schutzhund dog, it is critically important to choose a method you believe in and use it consistently. Many people will attend seminars given by trainers with various philosophies, and will switch their training method after each seminar they attend. Switching your training method every few months destroys a dog's confidence. Predictability is critically important to a dog. Although he can adapt to occasional changes in your style of training, he should not be expected to *constantly* adapt to changes in training.

It is your responsibility to learn a particular training system and then stick with it. Changing techniques within a given system is natural. This is why training is more of an art than a science. If it were a science, we could train all dogs in the exact same way and get the exact same results.

But because all dogs have variations in temperament, drives and personality, it takes an artful trainer to guide the dog into giving his best performance.

Still, changing techniques is not the same as moving from system to system. Therefore, we suggest that the Schutzhund enthusiast study as many different styles as are available and choose one that seems to be in line with his or her beliefs. Having done this, you need to stick to your guns and not allow another trainer or training director to step in and change the system, even temporarily. We have seen things done just once that have devastated dogs for the rest of their careers.

Developing a Training System

What is a system? A training system is how you go about training your dog, from step one all the way to competition at the highest levels. A training system is a philosophy on which you base your training; the basics should come from your own ethics and values.

Do you value your dog training for the time it allows you to spend with your dog, for the challenge of training and competition or for the sake of winning to boost your ego and prestige among your peers? This may be a brutally honest question, but before you truly establish a system to train your dog, you need to be honest with yourself and answer the question thoughtfully and truthfully—regardless of whether anyone else knows the answer.

Based on your answer to this question, you can choose a training system that will reflect your own personal style. You will know exactly how you intend to train your dog, and you will be committed to it and confident in your methods and approach.

You should be able to write down on paper what you wish to accomplish each day. Many trainers will step onto a field and at that very moment decide what they will do. This just wastes time and leads to training out of sequence (where the trainer remembers later that he or she should have covered a different lesson first), which will cause setbacks.

Having a training system and a specific goal for each session means you will accomplish the most you can in any given period of time. It means that you adhere to the *basics* in your system: This is the way you command, correct, praise and motivate your dog. Although you may use

Kelly Martin's A'Shane Ot Vitosha in first place at the 1998 DVG Nationals, and Martha Hoffman with Amok Ot Vitosha in third place. Both of these dogs were trained using our methods. (Beth Martin)

gimmicks here and there, the basis of your system should never vary. This should be the *constant technique* that your dog can rely upon.

The Right Dog

In any sport it is easiest to be competitive if you have the right equipment. In Schutzhund, that means having the right dog. In Chapter 2 we discussed the various options you face when choosing a Schutzhund candidate. The point we would like to make very clear in this conclusion is that *every dog does not make a good Schutzhund candidate*, regardless of his breed or his genetic heritage. Just because the dog is out of a Schutzhund III sire and dam does not *guarantee* the dog will be a good Schutzhund candidate.

Many times a dog has been forced to do Schutzhund routines when he does not have the natural ability or inclination. It is up to those more experienced in Schutzhund to advise the less experienced handlers when it is not worth pushing a certain dog through the exercises.

The dog that is right for Schutzhund *loves* the sport! The dog should be excited to carry out the majority of the exercises. If there are one or two that he has difficulty with, within reason, this is acceptable. But a dog that must be forced through all of the routines does not belong in Schutzhund.

All of us involved in Schutzhund should work together to keep dogs that do not belong in Schutzhund *off the field*. This means dogs that are unbalanced, both toward aggression and toward weakness. Either one can be a negative reflection on the sport.

Give Yourself Credit

Schutzhund is a difficult sport. It requires talent, diligence, commitment and those most cherished possessions—time and money.

Schutzhund is like a choreographed dance routine performed with a dog. Each element of the routine and how it should be performed is laid out, and then judged based on its correctness. Just as two people might learn to tango beautifully, step by step, the dog and handler do the same. The way you walk, how many steps you take, the way you turn, take and hold the dumbbell, and your other moves are all choreographed. Likewise, the way the dog moves, bites, retrieves, holds the dumbbell, downs in motion, performs the bark and hold, and does the other exercises are all choreographed.

This is difficult! It is worth saying again: Schutzhund is difficult. Because this is true, if you are committed to work in Schutzhund—and especially at the highest levels of Schutzhund—you deserve a pat on the back. "Good boy!" "Good girl!" What you are doing, either consciously or unconsciously, is synchronizing your mind, body and spirit with the mind, body and spirit of your dog. This demands a lot from both you and your dog. If one of these elements in either of you breaks down, you will not be able to function as a unit.

This is the synergy you must have to become a dynamic duo in the sport. This is the synergy it takes to become a team that competes in the Nationals and, ultimately, a team that represents their country in World competition.

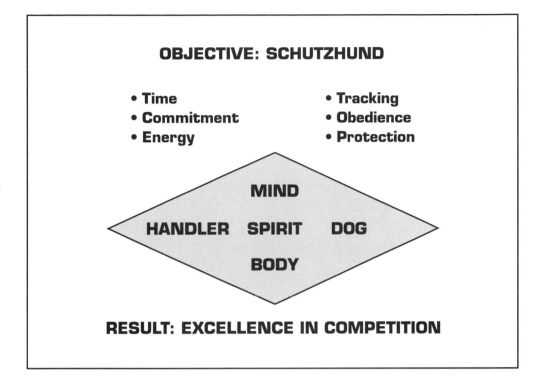

Schutzhund is a sport with many rewards. Most of those rewards are not monetary. They are more personal. The rewards are about your relationship with your dog, friendships formed, training lessons learned, lifestyles enlarged, competition enjoyed and opportunities to travel. As with any competition, Schutzhund requires commitment and sacrifice. But as anyone who has stood on the winner's platform for their country can attest, it is worth it!

We wish you and your canine partner many years of joy and rewarding training experiences. We hope to see you on that platform in the near future.

Glossary of Schutzhund Terminology

AD title   The endurance degree. The dog must trot beside his handler's bicycle for 12 miles. He must have sufficient stamina to do this in the allotted amount of time and then complete a few simple obedience exercises.

Article   The term used to describe a hand-sized personal object, such as a wallet, neutral in color, that is dropped on a track during a test after being handled by the track layer.

Bark and hold   The exercise in the protection phase of Schutzhund where the dog runs up to the helper in the blind and stands off the helper by barking at them in close proximity. The helper remains still.

Blind   The structure (permanent or portable) that the helper stands behind during the protection exercises in Schutzhund. The handler also hides behind it during the long down in the Schutzhund III exercise.

Civil agitation   Agitation that does not involve the use of artificial biting equipment such as sleeves or suits. The helper engages the dog in defense while wearing street clothes and using sticks, facial expressions, threatening movements and gestures.

Corrections The negative inducement given to the dog to supress an inappropriate response. A correction should never be applied to a dog that does not understand a command or is slow in learning.

Courage The willingness of the dog to subjugate his own personal safety in order to protect himself and/or his handler. Courage and fighting instinct are more than the dog being fearless. The dog must be willing to fight when threatened, even when the option to escape is present. In competition, the dog is awarded the rating of Pronounced, Sufficient or Not Sufficient.

Deep nose A desirable quality in tracking where the dog takes a full scent and tracks with his nose close to the ground.

Disposition The total characteristics of the dog's ability to perform what, according to his breed standard, he is intended to do.

Dumbbell An object with a cylinder in the center and two end pieces that is retrieved by the dog. The dumbbell is weighted according to the level at which the Schutzhund dog is working.

DVG (Deutcher Verband de Gebrauchshundsportvereine) German alliance for the utility dog sports.

Europameister World Champion Schutzhund III dog.

FH (Fahrtenhurd) The most advanced tracking title awarded by the SV. The dog must follow a stranger's track approximately 1,300 paces long and a minimum of three hours old. The track has four articles and is intersected by cross-tracks, laid by another stranger

Fuss The German command for "heel."

Hardness The dog's capacity to ignore unpleasant experiences during the protection phase and to demonstrate maximum courage and fighting spirit.

Hard sleeve A protective garment worn around the arm of the agitator. The hard sleeve is designed to protect the helper from injury when working with a particularly hard bite. It is usually constructed of hard leather and jute.

Heel Command in which the dog walks at the handler's left side with his shoulder in line with the handler's knee. The dog should not forge ahead or lag behind. The dog should automatically sit whenever the handler stops.

Helper   Also called agitator or decoy, this is the person used to sharpen or mold the dog's aggression. The helper is also used to stimulate aggression and teach the dog how to bite during the protection phase of the training.

Hier   The German command for "come."

High nose   A characteristic in tracking where the dog tracks with his nose too high off the ground. A dog with a high nose is using air scent as well as track scent and will lose points during the Schutzhund test.

Intelligence   The dog's ability to retain what he has learned and to profit from experience. This is an important trait in Schutzhund work.

Long line   A leash, approximately 30 feet long, used in all phases of Schutzhund training.

Motivation   The system of inducements given to promote desired behaviors. Praise, affection, food and toys all motivate.

OFA (Orthopedic Foundation for Animals)   A medical organization that rates a dog's hips as excellent, good or fair. When a dog receives an OFA number, he is certified to be free of hip dysplasia. An OFA number can only be issued after the dog is two years of age. The OFA also certifies elbows.

Platz   The German command for "down."

Revier   The bark and hold command in German.

Schutzhund   A dog sport originating in Germany that is designed to evaluate the dog's abilities in tracking, obedience and protection. The word means "protection dog" in German.

Sharpness   When the threshold for sensation in a dog is low, he will overreact to stimuli. This is called sharpness and is not a desired characteristic in Schutzhund. The dog is overly willing to engage in protection or may be a fear biter (called sharp shy).

Shyness   Generalized avoidance behavior that causes the dog to attempt to escape from a situation.

Sitz   The German command for "sit."

Sleeve   The protective covering over the arm of the helper during the protection phase.

Spirit   The zest and enthusiasm the dog shows for the work. A *very* desirable quality in Schutzhund.

Stick   A flexible, lightweight weapon used to evaluate the dog's ability to withstand a threat. A stick is not meant to inflict injury.

SV (Verein Für Deutsche Schæferhunde)   The German Shepherd Dog Club of Germany, founded by Max von Stephanitz.

Track scent   The scent left by a person, animal or object on the ground.

Trailing   A dog's habit of crossing back and forth over the track. This is an undesirable characteristic in Schutzhund.

Training collar   A collar that slips around the dog's neck, tightening with a correction and then loosening. This is also called a choke chain, and is the only acceptable collar in a Schutzhund trial.

USA (United Schutzhund Clubs of America)   The largest Schutzhund organization in America. It follows SV rules and regulations.

Viciousness   Unjustified aggression; biting without provocation.

Voran   The German term for the bark and hold in the blind.

Wall   The scaling or climbing jump that is part of Schutzhund II and III obedience routines.

Willingness   The dog's positive reaction to his handler's commands. The dog is enthusiastic and cheerful, even without reward.

Suggested Reading

Abrantes, Roger. *Dog Language: An Encyclopedia of Canine Behavior.* Naperville, IL: Wakan Tanka Publishers, 1996.

Barwig, Susan, and Stewart Hilliard. *Schutzhund Theory and Training Methods.* New York: Howell Book House, 1991.

Burch, Mary, and Jon Bailey. *How Dogs Learn.* New York: Howell Book House, 1999.

Duet, Karen Freeman, and George Duet. *The Home and Family Protection Dog.* New York: Howell Book House, 1993.

Duet, Karen Freeman, and George Duet. *The Business Security K-9.* New York: Howell Book House, 1995.

Lorenz, Konrad. *On Aggression.* New York: Fine Communications, 1997.

Reid, Pamela. *Excel-Erated Learning: Explaining How Dogs Learn and How Best to Teach Them.* Oakland, CA: James & Kenneth Publishing, 1996.

Schutzhund USA Rule Book. United Schutzhund Clubs of America, 3810 Paule Ave., St. Louis, MO 63125-1718, http://www.germanshepherddog.com.

About the Authors

Ivan Balabanov

I first got involved with dog training in 1982 in Bulgaria, when I went to the local dog training club and started learning and experimenting with teaching dogs. I began my dog training career with my Collie and a few German Shepherds. Eventually I discovered the Belgian Malinois, which I now breed in my own kennel, Ot Vitosha Kennels.

In Bulgaria I was training dogs for obedience and protection competitions when I got interested in Schutzhund. In 1985 I met Andre Vandergeten at a Schutzhund seminar in Czechoslovakia. He was already beginning to use a no-force approach to dog training. In 1988 I moved to Belgium to train dogs with him. This is when I got my first Belgian Malinois, Nakita Des Deux Pottois, SchIII, IPOIII, FH.

By the time I moved to the United States in 1991, I had adopted a similar no-force approach to dog training and had started to develop my own philosophy and training methods. In San Francisco I worked as a guide dog trainer for visually impaired people. Later I became a dog behaviorist at the San Francisco SPCA, working with a vast variety of dogs and behavior problems.

I started the Academy for Dog Trainers at the San Francisco SPCA. I now operate my own training business, Best Dogs Training Center.

Ivan Balabanov

Among the things I do are train and import police dogs, and give seminars on Schutzhund and Ring Sport.

I joined the United Schutzhund Clubs of America in 1991. I am also Training Director at both the Contra Costa Schutzhund Club and the San Francisco Ring Club.

I began competing regularly at national and regional events in 1992. I was the regional champion in 1995, and I've received the highest marks in all three phases of the competitions at national trials. I've competed at several world championships for Belgian Shepherds and at the FCI/IPO all-breed world championships. In both competitions I placed the highest ever for the U.S. team.

In the last few years, I have had the opportunity to train many dogs that I've bred. It is quite fulfilling to train such a dog with his handler, and seeing them go on to competitions and stand on the winner's platform is the ultimate reward. Since 1994 I have always had a dog of my breeding and training in the top 10 at national events. My accomplishments include:

- Regional champion, 1996
- USA Nationals, 1996, first place American bred and trained dog (high Obedience score in trial)
- DVG Nationals, 1997, third place (high Tracking in trial)
- Deutsche Meistershaft, 1997, sixth place (second highest Protection score in trial)

- DVG Nationals, 1998, first place (high Obedience, high Tracking scores in trial)
- DVG Nationals, 1998, third place

I also train dogs in Ring Sport. In 1997 I had a dog place first for American bred and trained. In 1998 I had the first American-bred and -trained dog to compete at the Mondioring World Championships. I also train dogs for personal protection, and one of my dogs has won several national protection tournaments.

If you are interested in finding out more, or to contact me, you can visit my Web site at www.malinois.com/otvitosha, or e-mail me at otvitosha@malinois.com.

Karen Freeman Duet

I am the founder and co-owner (along with my husband) of Kingsden's Kennels and K-9 Companions–K-9 Security and Detection International LLC. We, and our training staff, provide training for all breeds of dogs in obedience, problem solving and service dogs. We also provide home, family, and business protection to suitable dogs of stable temperament.

I'm also the author of two other Howell books: *The Home and Family Protection Dog* and *The Business Security K-9.* My husband and I also are trained security agents in our own right, holding the degree of PPS (Personal Protection Specialist) from The Executive Protection Institute, Berryville, Virginia. We provide protection for VIPs, celebrities and dignitaries, both

Karen Duet with C'Kimba Ot Vitosha

with and without K-9s. Our business is located in Lake Mathews (Riverside), California. You can contact us at (909) 780-5810, or K-9Cok-9Sec@webtv.net

I became involved in training in 1973, at age 12, with my Labrador Retriever. We competed in AKC obedience trials, earning the Companion Dog Excellent title. I became a professional trainer in 1979 when I became involved with Rottweilers and first discovered Schutzhund. I began to show and breed Rottweilers and compete with this breed, later producing Ch. Kingsden's Firestorm Dallas, Kingsden's L.A. Firestorm French Ring Brevet, and most recently Kingsden's Man O'War, along with many others. We currently breed Rottweilers, German Shepherds, Belgian Malinois and Bouviers.

I got involved in French Ring Sport when it first came to the United States in 1986, and I sponsored one of the first trainers from France to come to this country to teach the sport. He brought with him a three-month-old Belgian Malinois named Nany des Deux Pattois as a gift. Later, in 1991, I joined Schutzhund USA. Although Nana was well into Ring Sport, she would eventually receive her Schutzhund A, AD and BH degrees.

I met Ivan at the Schutzhund Nationals in 1993, where he was competing with Nakita des Deux Pottois, SchIII. At the trial, we found out we owned dogs that were full litter sisters. This was quite amazing, considering both dogs were born in Belgium!

Index

A

Abuse, 32
  correction and, 32
Acclimatization, 175
AD title, 189
Adult dog, selection of, 8, 15–17
A-frame jumps, 112
Aggression, 10, 15, 66, 130
Agitation. *See* Civil agitation and
    Helper
Air travel, 177–79
America Working Dog Federation
    (AWDF), 7
Anticipation, 22–23, 97, 115

article indication and, 57, 58–59
down command, 113–14
corner problems, 63
Anxiety (fearful reactions,
    nervousness), 61, 98, 108,
    146–47. *See also* Stress
gunshots and, 90–91
Articles, 40, 47
deductions, 44
defined, 189
fast trackers and, 49, 50, 51
indication of, 57–61
communication issues, 57–58
false, 58–59, 61
overshooting, 45, 59–60
materials of, 57, 59